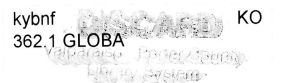

Global Health

Other Books in the Global Viewpoints Series

GLOBALVIEWPOINTS

| Global Health

Kathryn Roberts, Book Editor

GREENHAVEN PUBLISHING

Published in 2020 by Greenhaven Publishing, LLC
353 3rd Avenue, Suite 255, New York, NY 10010

First Edition

Articles in Greenhaven Publishing anthologies are often edited for length to meet page
requirements. In addition, original titles of these works are changed to clearly present
the main thesis and to explicitly indicate the author's opinion. Every effort is made to
ensure that Greenhaven Publishing accurately reflects the original intent of the authors.
Every effort has been made to trace the owners of the copyrighted material.

Cover image: Valeriya Anufriyeva/Shutterstock.com, © Can Stock Photo/
Volokhatiuk (clouds), © Tsiumpa/Dreamstime.com (Earth)

Map: frees/Shutterstock.com

Cataloging-in-Publication Data

Names: Roberts, Kathryn, editor.
Title: Global health / Kathryn Roberts, book editor.
Description: First edition. | New York : Greenhaven Publishing, 2020. | Series: Global
viewpoints | Includes bibliographical references and index. | Audience: Grades 9-12.
Identifiers: ISBN 9781534506473 (library binding) | ISBN 9781534506466 (paperback)
Subjects: LCSH: World health—Juvenile literature. | Public health—Juvenile literature.
Classification: LCC RA432.G563 2020 | DDC 362.1—dc23

Manufactured in the United States of America

Website: http://greenhavenpublishing.com

Contents

Chapter 1: What Are the Biggest Threats to Health Around the World?

Chapter 2: What Impact Does Fake News Have on Global Health?

Chapter 3: What Are the Causes of the Rise of Mental Health Disorders Around the World?

Chapter 4: What Has Impacted Women's Health Around the World?

countries seeking safe abortions and other much needed medical services.

Foreword

Global interdependence has become an undeniable reality. Mass media and technology have increased worldwide access to information and created a society of global citizens. Understanding and navigating this global community is a challenge, requiring a high degree of information literacy and a new level of learning sophistication.

Building on the success of its flagship series, Opposing Viewpoints, Greenhaven Publishing has created the Global Viewpoints series to examine a broad range of current, often controversial topics of worldwide importance from a variety of international perspectives. Providing students and other readers with the information they need to explore global connections and think critically about worldwide implications, each Global Viewpoints volume offers a panoramic view of a topic of widespread significance.

Drugs, famine, immigration—a broad, international treatment is essential to do justice to social, environmental, health, and political issues such as these. Junior high, high school, and early college students, as well as general readers, can all use Global Viewpoints anthologies to discern the complexities relating to each issue. Readers will be able to examine unique national perspectives while, at the same time, appreciating the interconnectedness that global priorities bring to all nations and cultures.

Material in each volume is selected from a diverse range of sources, including journals, magazines, newspapers, nonfiction books, speeches, government documents, pamphlets, organization newsletters, and position papers. Global Viewpoints is truly global, with material drawn primarily from international sources available in English and secondarily from U.S. sources with extensive international coverage.

Features of each volume in the Global Viewpoints series include:

- An **annotated table of contents** that provides a brief summary of each essay in the volume, including the name of the country or area covered in the essay.

- An **introduction** specific to the volume topic.

- A world map to help readers locate the countries or areas covered in the essays.

- For each viewpoint, **an introduction** that contains notes about the author and source of the viewpoint explains why material from the specific country is being presented, summarizes the main points of the viewpoint, and offers three **guided reading questions** to aid in understanding and comprehension.

- **For further discussion** questions that promote critical thinking by asking the reader to compare and contrast aspects of the viewpoints or draw conclusions about perspectives and arguments.

- A worldwide list of **organizations to contact** for readers seeking additional information.

- A **periodical bibliography** for each chapter and a **bibliography of books** on the volume topic to aid in further research.

- A comprehensive **subject index** to offer access to people, places, events, and subjects cited in the text.

Global Viewpoints is designed for a broad spectrum of readers who want to learn more about current events, history, political science, government, international relations, economics, environmental science, world cultures, and sociology— students doing research for class assignments or debates, teachers and faculty seeking to supplement course materials, and others wanting to understand current issues better. By presenting how people in various countries perceive the root causes, current consequences, and proposed solutions to worldwide challenges, Global Viewpoints volumes offer readers opportunities to enhance their global awareness and their knowledge of cultures worldwide.

Introduction

Around the world, countries have seen their fair share of medical tragedies and triumphs in recent years. Some of these medical hurdles are new, like in 2016 when the sports world was rocked by the potential issues caused by the rapid spread of Zika Virus in South America, specifically in the Olympic-host country of Brazil. It was debated whether Rio de Janeiro, which faced some of the highest rates of the Zika Virus, would be a fit host for the games, not just because of the way the country was handling the spread of the virus, but also because competitors from other countries would potentially carry the virus to their home nations upon completion of the Olympics. Would countries without access to advancements in medical care, such as Nigeria and Ghana, be able to deal with the crisis?

But some of these medical hurdles have been around a long time. African nations have long since been the focus when it comes to the treatment and eradication efforts of HIV and AIDS. While the efforts to lower the transmission of HIV have been successful since the pandemic's origins in the 1980s, there is still much work to be done to provide access to those who need medication, treatment, and most importantly, the education on how sexually transmitted infections like HIV can be passed from person to person.

Through the clear connection between economic instability and the spread of disease, countries like the Dominican Republic and Haiti see the struggle to lower their maternal mortality rates but have been unable to provide adequate care to mothers who have not had the opportunities to see doctors until late into their often high-risk pregnancies.

But what about when the government is to blame? In countries like Syria, where civil war has raged for years, the Syrian government has been one of the greatest causes of health crises by using local civilian hospitals as a weapon of war. With regular attacks on hospitals, and the number of local medical professionals diminishing, Syrian civilians have been unable to seek the medical attention that they require, which furthers the instability in the region.

Additionally, the rise in celebrity-spread fake medical news has caused doctors to revisit the ways in which they can make medical information easier to access and understand for their patients. While some celebrities have led to positive medical news stories, like actress and activist Angelina Jolie shining a light on rare forms of breast cancer, it cannot be emphasized enough that people should heed the advice of medical professionals such as their personal physicians, who can provide diagnoses that are custom to their patients' needs. Not only that, but when it comes to children and vaccines, the fraudulent paper showing an unfounded connection between the MMR vaccine and autism has caused the resurgence of many eradicated diseases, most often due to celebrities perpetuating the idea that children should not be properly immunized.

And then there are the international stigmas surrounding mental health. India, which has recently been deemed one of the most depressed countries in the world, sees over thirty-eight million people dealing with depression, but only a few thousand psychiatrists and psychologists practicing in the country, and only able to practice in the more urban areas. With a rash of under- and mis-reporting, the actual numbers of men and women impacted by diagnosable mental health disorders around the world is unknown, but it is likely that 18 percent of men and women in the United States have suffered through some form of mental illness.

While it is easy to point out everything wrong in the world, it is important to also measure the actions taken to advance healthcare internationally. In Haiti, following the destructive earthquake in 2010 and the spike of cases of post-traumatic stress disorder (PTSD) organizations are customizing the ways they treat cases, leading to more ways that these efforts can be made right after tragedies strike, rather than months and months later. With advancements in technology, new therapies are being approved, including gene therapies and state-of-the-art vaccines. Even the ways in which people receive medications have improved with the advancements in drone technology.

In *Global Viewpoints: Global Health* diverse perspectives from writers around the world examine the most important issue facing each one of us. In chapters titled "What Are the Biggest Threats to Health Around the World?," "What Impact Does Fake News Have on Global Health?," "What Are the Causes of the Rise of Mental Health Disorders Around the World?," and "What Has Impacted Women's Health Around the World?," readers will learn about the efforts made in countries around the world to innovate and expand the reach of lifesaving and life-improving measures in both physical and mental health.

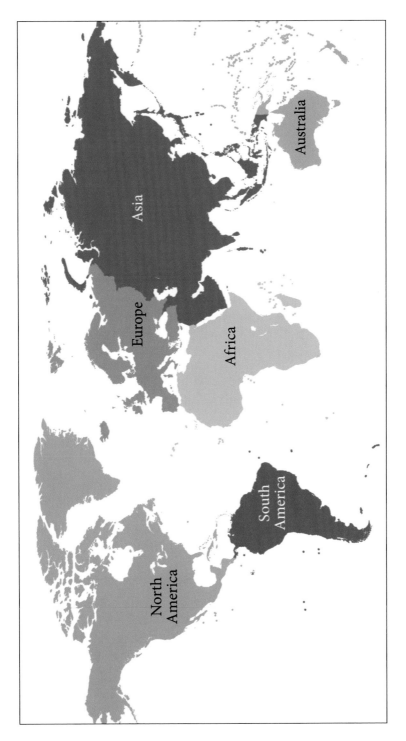

CHAPTER 1

What Are the Biggest Threats to Health Around the World?

In Europe Climate Change Is Affecting Public Health

Bettina Menne

In the following viewpoint Bettina Menne addresses the impacts climate change has on public health in Europe. Extreme weather that results from climate change has been responsible for an increasing number of deaths throughout Europe. Secondary problems, such as loss of homes, stress, disease, and pollution of air and water, also take a toll on the health of the population. The author argues that governments and leaders must take measures to protect public health, since extreme weather events are unlikely to decrease. Bettina Menne is programme manager at WHO Europe.

As you read, consider the following questions:

1. How many climate change-related deaths per year worldwide does the WHO estimate by the year 2040?
2. What types of extreme weather have compromised health in Europe, according to the author?
3. What is "active transport" and how can it help mitigate both climate change and health risks?

Climate change affects public health in many different ways. There are direct and indirect impacts, as well as those that occur immediately and those that occur over a longer period of

"Climate Changes and Human Health," by Bettina Menne, European Environment Agency, June 30, 2015. https://www.eea.europa.eu/signals/signals-2015/interviews/climate-change-and-human-health. Licensed under CC BY 2.5 DK.

time. We estimate that 150,000 deaths worldwide were caused by climate change in 2000. According to a new WHO study, this is projected to increase to 250,000 deaths per year worldwide by 2040. This estimate would have actually been higher if we had not factored in the reduction of child mortality expected in future years.

Extreme weather events are already among the top climate-change impacts that affect public health. In addition, mortality related to heatwaves and flooding is expected to increase, in particular in Europe. And changes in the distribution of vector-borne diseases will also affect human health.

How Do Extreme Weather Events Affect Public Health?

Different types of extreme weather events affect different regions. Heatwaves are mostly a problem in southern Europe and the Mediterranean, but they are also a problem in other regions. According to estimates, the heatwave of 2003 caused 70,000 excess deaths in 12 European countries, mostly among older people. As people get older, the thermal regulation of the body is impaired, which makes older people more vulnerable to high temperatures.

By 2050, heatwaves are projected to cause 120,000 excess deaths per year in the European Union, and to have an economic cost of EUR 150 billion if no further measures are taken. This higher estimate is not only due to more frequent and higher temperatures but also due to Europe's changing demographics. Currently, around 20% of EU citizens are over 65 years of age, and their share in the population is expected to increase to around 30% in 2050.

High temperatures are also often associated with air pollution, and ground-level ozone pollution in particular. Air pollution can cause respiratory and cardiovascular problems, especially among children and older people, and can result in premature deaths.

Other extreme weather events—such as high precipitation events that might cause floods—also affect public health.

How Do Floods Affect Our Health?

To give a concrete example, the devastating floods in 2014 in Bosnia and Herzegovina, Croatia, and Serbia caused 60 deaths and affected more than 2.5 million people. In addition to the immediate health impacts, rescue operations and public health services were also affected. Many hospitals, especially lower floors where heavy medical equipment is often kept, were flooded. This reduced the capacity of health services to cope with the disaster and to care for existing patients.

In the aftermath of such a disaster, displaced people who lost their homes are also likely to suffer from other long-term health problems, including stress.

There are also indirect health risks, largely due to deterioration or contamination of the environment. For example, floods can carry pollutants and chemicals from industrial facilities, waste water, and sewage water. This can lead to the contamination of drinking water and agricultural land. When there is no secure faecal and chemical disposal, floodwaters or greater run off can carry contaminants to lakes and the sea, and some might enter our food chain.

What Other Kinds of Health Risks Are Associated with Climate Change?

The health risks come from a variety of sources. Higher temperatures facilitate forest fires. Around 70,000 forest fires occur every year on the European continent. Although the large majority are man-made, high temperatures and droughts often worsen the overall damage. While some fires might result in loss of lives and property, they all cause air pollution, especially from particulate matter. This in turns triggers illness and premature death.

Higher temperatures, milder winters, and wetter summers are expanding the area where certain disease-carrying insects (such as ticks and mosquitoes) can survive and thrive. These insects can then carry diseases—such as Lyme disease, dengue, and malaria—to new areas where the climate was not suitable to the disease previously.

Climate change could also mean that some diseases might no longer be able to thrive in the areas they currently affect. For example, future warming could mean that ticks—and consequently tick-borne diseases—will be found at higher altitudes and further north, closely linked to the changing distribution of their natural hosts, such as deer.

Seasonal variations—some seasons starting earlier and lasting longer—might also have adverse impacts on human health. This could have a particular effect on people with allergies. We might also experience peaks in asthma cases, triggered by combined exposure to different allergens at the same time.

There are also other long-term health risks associated with climate change. Changes in temperature and precipitation are expected to affect food-production capacity in the wider pan-European region, with significant reductions expected in Central Asia. A further reduction of production capacity in the region could not only exacerbate the malnutrition problem, but also could have widespread impacts by raising food prices worldwide. Climate change is therefore a factor we have to take into account when we look at food security and access to affordable food. It can aggravate existing social and economic problems.

How Can Public Authorities Prepare for the Health Impacts of Climate Change?

Compared with many other regions, European health services are relatively better equipped to deal with the health impacts of climate change. Malaria, for example, is not likely to re-establish itself in the European Union. Nevertheless, single events such as floods or long-lasting heatwaves will continue to exert increasing pressure on the health services in affected areas. European countries will need to strengthen and adapt their health services to cope with the potential impacts of climate change in their area. Some measures could involve relocating and refitting hospitals to prepare against possible floods. Other measures could include better tools for sharing information with vulnerable groups to prevent their exposure to pollution.

WHO Europe has been working on the health effects of climate change for more than 20 years. We develop methods and tools, carry out impact assessments, and provide assistance to Member States to adapt to climate change. In our recent report, we recommend adaptation measures, but we stress that adaptation measures will not be enough on their own.

It is quite clear that countries also need to undertake measures to mitigate climate change to protect public health. Some of these measures can have significant health co-benefits. For example, the promotion of so-called "active transport" (such as cycling and walking) can contribute to reducing obesity and non-communicable diseases. And renewable energy such as solar energy can help to provide continuous energy to health services in remote areas.

HIV: It's Time to Recalibrate and Target the Weak Spots

Linda-Gail Bekker

In the following viewpoint, Linda-Gail Bekker details the strides that have been made since the HIV/AIDS epidemic began in the late 1980s—including twenty-two million people currently living on lifesaving antiretroviral treatments. But the current pace is insufficient to meet the global goal of ending HIV by 2030. With the emphasis on treatment and prevention, populations like men who have sex with men, women in the sex trade, and drug users have been left behind, Bekker points out that those vulnerable populations need to be included in any further plans to attack the disease. Additionally, with the number of men who have HIV in South Africa, efforts must be made to get those not currently in health services the proper treatment they require. Linda-Gail Bekker is professor of medicine and deputy director of the Desmond Tutu HIV Centre at the Institute of Infectious Disease and Molecular Medicine, University of Cape Town.

As you read, consider the following questions:

1. According to the viewpoint, what is one of the primary ways to limit the transmission of HIV, and why is it important that this method be emphasized?
2. Why have regions in Eastern Europe and Central Asia seen a 30 percent increase in new HIV infections since 2010?
3. Why would decriminalizing sex work in South Africa lower the likelihood of the spread of HIV?

HIV remains a global challenge. Between 36.7 million and 38.8 million people live with the disease worldwide. And more than 35 million have died of AIDS related causes since the start of the epidemic in the mid-1980s. Two years ago the International Aids Society and The Lancet put together a commission made up of a panel of experts to take stock and identify what the future response to HIV should be. The report is being released to coincide with the 22nd International Aids Conference in Amsterdam. The Conversation Africa's Health and Medicine Editor Candice Bailey spoke to Head of the International AIDS Society Professor Linda-Gail Bekker, who also led the commission, about its report.

What have we learnt about the global HIV response in the last 30 years?

The world had an emergency on its hands 30 years ago with the arrival of HIV. A huge amount of effort was put into trying to find solutions. And there were some incredible breakthroughs. First was the miracle of lifesaving antiretroviral treatment, the biggest game changer over the last three decades. Great strides have been made in rolling out the treatment. UNAIDS tells us that 22 million people are currently on treatment. That's truly remarkable.

But we've also learnt that relying on the current pace is insufficient. That's clear from the figures. In some countries the incidence is rising, and in many parts of the world the incidence rate has stalled or plateaued. We are not seeing the downturn that we need to be able to reach the global goal of ending the HIV pandemic by 2030.

The biggest lesson we've learnt is that we need to reinvigorate the prevention message especially since we have new tools to combat HIV transmission in many different settings. This includes Pre-exposure prophylaxis (PrEP)—a daily antiretroviral that's given to people who have a high risk of contracting HIV to lower their chances of getting infected—as well as treatment as prevention, which involves giving people living with HIV antiretrovirals to suppress their viral loads.

For a sustainable response and looking forward to the next era, it will be important to position our responses to HIV within the broader health agenda. Patients don't only have HIV, they have other issues. There are mental health needs and there are sexual and reproductive health needs, so HIV treatment and care must fit into that broader agenda. This will enable a more sustainable response.

This is a challenge in many parts of the world where HIV is in a siloed response and people are only treated by HIV specific services. There needs to be a service delivery model that considers the broader health agenda. This goes beyond integration. We need to think about where can we take the lessons from HIV into other diseases. In the case of HIV, person centred and community-based care has become critical to ensure people get access to treatment.

The message is simple: the epidemic is far from over and it's not time to disengage. We're here for the long haul. To ensure we have a sustainable approach we need to recalibrate.

The commission is calling for a new way of doing business that will seek common cause with other global health issues. We understand that the HIV response will need resources. This will be a great way to get a double bang for the buck.

Health Challenges Resulting from the Global Refugee Crisis

The overwhelming burden of hosting the now 60 million forcibly displaced people worldwide has for decades fallen on the developing world, with 86 per cent of the total being cared for in low- and middle-income countries. With the physical impacts of this growing global crisis now spilling into in the developed world, the issue—including aspects related to health—has rapidly ascended the global political agenda.

Significant to note from a health perspective is that there is no systematic association between refugee migration and the importation of infectious diseases. There is also no clear evidence of benefits of obligatory border screening for infectious diseases like tuberculosis. Nor have there been any significant outbreaks of infectious disease linked to the hundreds of thousands of refugees that have arrived in Europe since the start of the current crisis (over 850,000 have crossed the Mediterranean since January 2015). Mass movements of people do carry some health risks. But collective health security in relation to refugees is better understood as a danger of socioeconomic inequality.

Freed from rhetoric, health risks among refugees are minimal in most cases, or significant but manageable in others. For example, strong vaccine surveillance systems in Germany quickly detected measles immunization uptake rates as below optimal among incoming refugees to Lower Saxony and measures are already in place to vaccinate arriving groups.

High-income countries have both the institutional strength and the innovative capacity to find cost and clinically effective solutions to health challenges that might arise from the inward migration and also the ability to harness its socioeconomic opportunities and benefits. For example, the use of social outreach models of care and of mobile screening units in East London showed them to be clinically- and cost- effective in finding and treating hard to reach cases of tuberculosis. Conceivably, given this is a crisis of large mobile populations across Europe, the role of mobile diagnostic units that have an integrated support function for psychosocial care (e.g. a psychiatric nurse) may provide a cost-effective option for monitoring and addressing health needs as the refugee crisis evolves.

"Facing the Health Challenges of the Global Refugee Crisis," by Abbas Omaar, Dr. Osman Dar and Professor Ali Zumla, Chatham House, November 30, 2015.

What's still going wrong?

In many regions we have left whole sectors of the population behind. These include men who have sex with men, women who trade sex and people who inject drugs. They aren't getting proper services because of policy, prejudice and stigma.

And different regional pockets need particular attention. One is in Eastern Europe and Central Asia where there has been a 30% increase in new infections since 2010. This is particularly concerning. Its clear that whole regions are being left behind because of politics, denial and stigma.

Here the administrations are not doing the evidence based thing—they are failing their people and the response.

Another pocket is West and Central Africa. These are countries that are not reducing rates of infection as quickly as we had hoped, often due to limited resources. Nigeria, for example, needs help with the reduction of mother to child transmission.

These are areas that are going to need attention, help and encouragement.

But we don't want to put out the notion that we are in trouble across the world.

In East and South Africa, for example, we have made significant gains. There is still a lot to be done but the trends are going in the right direction. In many ways South Africa really is a good news story because its administration and politics favour an enthusiastic response to do the right thing. Domestic funding around HIV has increased. South Africa still has the biggest number of people in the world living with HIV—7.9 million according to the latest HSRC report. But the country is beginning to turn the ship around. That's something we can be incredibly proud of.

There are, nevertheless, still pockets that need attention. For example, adolescent girls and young women under the age of 25 in KwaZulu-Natal are roughly three times more likely than men younger than 25 to be living with HIV. We have had them in our sights but we now need a concentrated effort to tackle HIV in this cohort otherwise we will miss the target.

We need to look at the evidence and where can we make an impact with integrated care. This would be through HIV programmes that are part of sexual and reproductive health along with economic empowerment initiatives such as getting girls to stay in school and making sure they have opportunities to make autonomous decisions about sexual and reproductive health.

Doing everything for everyone is a waste of money and time. We need to sharpen the tip of our response. We must put our responses where we get the biggest bang for buck and call on those resources that offer prevention and treatment.

What are the biggest challenges between now and 2030?

Resources are the constant challenge globally. We live in a world where politics is unpredictable. We need to constantly advocate for funding while diversifying funding opportunities.

The second challenge is stigma and discrimination. Policy and ideology that is counter productive also feeds into stigma and discrimination. We need to do to something about laws that criminalise behaviour, like sex work, and stigmas towards intravenous drug users, gay people and men who have sex with men. Decriminalising sex work in South Africa, for example, would go a long way to reduce stigma, enable services and help the public health approach.

Continuing to understand how to reach young women and girls and protect them socially and medically; those are also big challenges.

Finally, in South Africa there is a challenge to find men who are not in the health services and get them into care and onto treatment. We know that a suppressed viral load means no HIV transmission and so this should be on its agenda.

In Brazil Zika Virus Threatens the Olympics

Ashifa Kassam

In the following viewpoint, Ashifa Kassam details the one of the more famous, not-entirely-political struggles the country of Brazil faced in 2016 prior to hosting the Summer Olympics in Rio de Janeiro. Leading up to the Olympics, Rio de Janeiro reported the highest number of suspected cases of Zika at 26,000 or 157 per 100,000—the fourth highest in the country. While many people infected with the virus would not have many symptoms—the worst would be closely related to the flu—the biggest impact of Zika was on pregnant women, as the virus has been proven to cause severe birth defects, including abnormally small heads and underdeveloped brains. Ashifa Kasam is the Canada correspondent for Guardian US.

As you read, consider the following questions:

1. Why was Brazil most impacted by the Zika virus?
2. What was one of the greatest concerns about hosting the Olympics during the Zika epidemic?
3. Ultimately, why did the International Olympic Committee decide to not postpone or move the Rio Olympics in 2016?

"Zika Virus Makes Rio Olympics a Threat in Brazil and Abroad, Health Expert Says," by Ashifa Kassam, Guardian News and Media Limited, May 12, 2016. https://www. theguardian.com/world/2016/may/12/rio-olympics-zika-amir-attaran-public-health-threat. Reprinted by permission.

As Brazil reels from a spiraling political crisis and its deepest recession in decades, a public health specialist in Canada has added to the country's woes with a high-profile call for the 2016 summer Olympics—slated to kick off in Rio de Janeiro in early August—to be postponed or moved due to the Zika outbreak.

"But for the Games, would anyone recommend sending an extra half a million visitors into Brazil right now?" Canadian professor Amir Attaran, whose research areas include population health and global development policy, asked this week in a commentary published in the Harvard Public Health Review.

First seen in Brazil last year, the Zika virus has now been detected in more than 50 countries. Brazil remains the country most-affected by the mosquito-borne virus, which has been proven to cause a severe birth defect that results in babies born with abnormally small heads and underdeveloped brains. The virus has also been linked to Guillain-Barré syndrome, a rare neurological disorder that can result in paralysis and death.

In February, the World Health Organization declared the Zika virus a public health emergency of international concern. Save for advising pregnant women not to travel to Zika-affected areas—including Rio de Janeiro—WHO has not issued any other travel restrictions on Zika-affected countries.

Speaking to the *Guardian* on Thursday, Attaran described the idea of going ahead with the games as both "indescribably foolish" and "monstrously unethical". The potential risks to visitors range from brain-damaged children to death in rare instances, he added. "Is this what the Olympics stand for?"

The state of Rio de Janeiro has recorded 26,000 suspected Zika cases—the highest of any state in Brazil—and has an incident rate of 157 per 100,000, the fourth highest in the country, he said. "What is proposed is to bring half a million Olympic visitors into the heart of the epidemic."

The deluge of athletes and visitors expected to pour into Rio from countries around the world could facilitate the virus's transmission in countries that to date have been unaffected, he said.

The risk is that the virus may land on the doorstep of countries that do not have adequate healthcare infrastructure to tackle the virus. "With all those skills and gifts that Brazil possesses, it has been unable to quell this catastrophe," said Attaran. "Are we seriously expecting that Nigeria, the Congo, and Indonesia will be able to do so?"

On Thursday, WHO responded to the claims, noting that the Zika virus usually results in mild symptoms—ranging from fever, body aches and rashes—with most of those affected not experiencing any symptoms at all.

The organisation said it has been working with the Brazilian government to mitigate the risk posed by Zika to athletes and visitors, and is encouraging visitors to take precautions to protect themselves from mosquito bites and practice safer sex.

The timing of the Games may also prove help helpful. "The Games will take place during Brazil's wintertime when there are fewer active mosquitoes and the risk of being bitten is lower," the organisation said in a statement.

The International Olympic Committee said it has no plans to postpone or move the Games and instead has been in close contact with WHO to track the Zika virus in Brazil. "We are working with our partners in Rio on measures to deal with the pools of stagnant

---

Climate Change and Global Health

Warmer conditions linked to climate change are enlarging the potential range of mosquito-borne diseases such as dengue fever as well as other health threats, the report said.

Since 1950, the Baltic region has seen a 24-percent increase in coastal areas suitable for cholera outbreaks, while in sub-Saharan Africa's highlands, zones where malaria-carrying mosquitoes can survive have expanded by 27 percent.

Hotter conditions may also be giving some disease-causing microbes greater resistance to antibiotics, Salas said.

And higher temperatures seem to be curbing the maximum harvest from farmland in all regions of the world, reversing an earlier trend toward ever-larger harvests, the report noted. Ebi, of the University of Washington, said rising carbon dioxide levels in the atmosphere are shrinking nutrients in cereal crops, hiking the risk of malnutrition even for those who get enough to eat.

Mental health threats, meanwhile—from children worried about their future in an overheating world to families stressed by disaster losses—are on the rise, she said.

Acting swiftly to curb climate change—whether by switching to clean energy, or getting more people to walk and use bicycles—would lower healthcare costs by the same amount of money needed to reduce emissions, Ebi said.

"Most mitigation policies are good for health—and they're good for health now," she said.

"Why Climate Change Is the Biggest Global Health Threat of the Century,"
by Laurie Goering, World Economic Forum, November 29, 2018.

---

water around the Olympic venues, where the mosquitos breed, to minimise the risk of visitors coming into contact with them," the IOC told the Guardian.

In recent weeks, the Zika outbreak has been eclipsed by the many challenges facing Brazil: Dilma Rousseff, the country's president, has been stripped of her presidential duties and is facing impeachment; the economy has plunged into a deep recession;

and uproar has been growing over a corruption scandal involving the state-controlled oil company, Petrobras, and politicians across the spectrum.

Rousseff was suspended early on Thursday, after the country's senate voted to impeach her over charges she whitewashed government finances. Hours later the interim president, Michael Temer, named a politician with no medical background as the new health minister. The portfolio will be taken by Ricardo Barros, a civil engineer by training. He is the fourth health minister in little more than half a year.

The medical director of Australia's Olympic team said he believed the risk of the Zika virus was minimal for Australian athletes. "The last couple of people that I have spoken to, who have been to Rio in the past month or two, haven't seen a mosquito," said David Hughes in a statement. "Given that there is no chance that the Games are going to be shifted to another venue, I believe we can proceed with confidence, knowing that we have appropriate guidelines and preventative measures in place."

Canada's Attaran is not the first academic to publicly question whether the games in Brazil should go on as planned. In February, New York University's Arthur Caplan and Lee Igel, wrote in an article that "to host the Games at a site teeming with Zika ... is, quite simply, irresponsible".

Attaran pointed to the 1976 Winter Olympics—moved to Austria after mounting costs forced the American city of Denver to withdraw as host—as a precedent for allowing the Games to be changed in exceptional circumstances. "I'm not the Olympic Grinch. I'm not calling for the games to be cancelled," he said. "What I'm asking for is a bit of delayed gratification so that babies aren't born permanently disabled."

In Puerto Rico a Natural Disaster Exacerbates Food Shortage and Poor Health Care

Lauren Lluveras

In the following viewpoint, Lauren Lluveras—a daughter of Puerto Rican immigrants—details the concerns facing the island in the wake of Hurricane Maria, which hit in September 2017. Following Puerto Rico's declaration of bankruptcy in May 2017, the island was hit by the natural disaster, which severely impacted its ability to import food, as those foods most often came from countries also hit by Maria. Roughly 80 percent of the island's crop value vanished overnight after the hurricane, a loss of approximately $780 million in food. Additionally, 45 percent of the population lives in poverty and relies on public transit to get around, which was unavailable after the hurricane. Lauren Lluveras is a postdoctoral fellow at the Institute for Urban Policy Research and Analysis at the University of Texas at Austin.

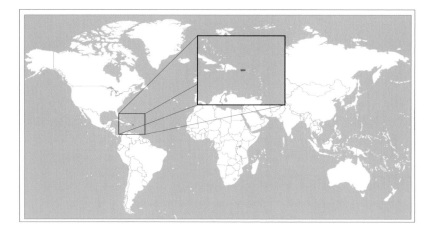

As you read, consider the following questions:

1. Why do certain groups in the United States want to forget that the people who live in Puerto Rico are US citizens and should be treated like citizens from any other state?
2. What are the complications that would impact Puerto Rico's recovery from Hurricane Maria?
3. How does a loss of power impact Puerto Rico's already fragile healthcare system?

The United States had already seen its share of disasters, from back-to-back hurricanes that devastated Texas, Florida and the U.S. Virgin Islands to roaring wildfires in the West.

Then, after battering the rest of the Caribbean, Hurricane Maria left the island of Puerto Rico facing a humanitarian crisis. About a dozen people died in the Sept. 21 storm and the island was plunged into darkness.

Now, some 3.4 million Puerto Ricans—which is to say, 3.4 million American citizens—are confronting life without electricity, gas, cellular service and, in many cases, a home.

After a decade of fiscal decline and a May 2017 bankruptcy, Puerto Rico has become exceptionally vulnerable to disasters like Maria. As both a policy analyst and the daughter of Puerto Rican immigrants, I'm concerned about how austerity-related reforms are now threatening the survival of not just my family there but everyone on the island.

Though food insecurity, poor health care and resource-starved public transit all predate the hurricane, the result of both damaging U.S. policy and deepening financial crisis, these three problems will dramatically complicate Puerto Rico's recovery.

Food Insecurity

Because Puerto Rico imports over 85 percent of its food, food security on the island has always been fragile. The U.S. territory has been rationing supplies since Hurricane Irma in early September, but according to Puerto Rico's former secretary of agriculture, it may have just one month's worth of food on hand.

Puerto Rico's main port reopened Sept. 23, allowing 11 ships to begin arriving with aid and resources, including clean water and food. Even so, distributing supplies across the 3,515-square-mile island will prove difficult on roadways damaged by flooding, debris and downed power lines.

Puerto Rico's food supply is also uncertain given that several islands from which it imports food, including the Dominican Republic, Dominica and St. Martin, were also hit hard. And if the island goes without power for up to six months, the shelf life of the meat, vegetables, fruit and other staples of the traditionally fresh Puerto Rican diet will be awfully short.

This is the U.S. territory's second food shortage in recent years. When a Puerto Rico-bound cargo vessel, El Faro, sank during Hurricane Joaquin in 2015, residents spent months in strife as the government struggled to develop a plan that ensured everyone had enough to eat.

Prior to World War II, Puerto Rico actually had an agricultural economy, producing and exporting sugar cane, tobacco and citrus fruits. But, post-war industrialization and growing stigma around farm work led to a downturn. Today, the island can't feed its populace or compete with developed countries' agribusiness and cheap prices.

In response, Puerto Rico has made an effort to grow domestic food production, which has increased 24 percent in the past five years. But Maria's winds and floodwaters demolished these gains in bananas, plantains, coffee, dairy and corn production. Roughly 80 percent of Puerto Rico's crop value just vanished over night, a loss of approximately US$780 million.

Poor Health Care

Puerto Rico had poor health care before Hurricanes Irma and Maria, but the storms will exacerbate this desperate situation, too. Ravaged by austerity, hospitals and other health care facilities saw their budgets cut by 15 percent from 2011 to 2015. Countless public clinics across the island closed during the past year, while four hospitals have filed for bankruptcy.

The island is also short on health care professionals, with 72 percent of Puerto Rico's 78 municipalities deemed "medically underserved."

This deficient system will face grave challenges in providing medical care to Puerto Ricans injured during and after the storm. Serious cuts and broken bones are extremely common following hurricanes, as are heat-related and infectious illnesses.

Loss of power may also lead to the worsening of illnesses for residents with such chronic conditions as diabetes, heart disease, psychiatric disorders and HIV whose medications require refrigeration. My own abuela (grandmother), a diabetic who began having mild cardiac episodes last year, is one Puerto Rican among thousands in this situation.

These domestic barriers to medical care are magnified by the ongoing debate around health care in the U.S. Even though Puerto Rico residents are more likely to be poor, elderly and diagnosed with a chronic illness than the general population, caps to Medicaid reimbursements have forced several hospitals on the island to cut services, close wings, leave positions unfilled and reduce employee hours and pay.

In the wake of this natural disaster, experts expect Puerto Rico's hospitals to be overburdened, especially in San Juan and other metropolitan areas, where most medical facilities are located. In recent days, Gov. Ricardo Roselló has resorted to retweeting information about which hospitals are open and receiving patients.

Transportation Shortages

Many Puerto Ricans will not be able to reach help, though. Upwards of 45 percent of the population lives in poverty and an estimated 35,000 riders depend daily on public transit to get around.

With a limited budget, an aging infrastructure and too few vehicles to support the island's population, however, the transit authority has been struggling to meet needs. The agency underwent austerity-related budget cuts in 2015, operating at a deficit until, finally, in May 2017, it filed for bankruptcy.

This history has complicated evacuation efforts. Locals were puzzled at the "leave or die" warnings sent to Isabela residents on Sept. 23 when a large crack in the Guajataca dam threatened to flood surrounding areas. How, exactly, were they supposed to leave? And how could they get out on roadways long since rendered impassable?

As rescue and recovery efforts continue, transportation shortages have effectively left many residents reachable only by helicopter.

People across the island are already suffering the consequences. One family—Irees Gonzalez Collazo, 74, and her two sisters, Carmen, 73, and Sara, 72, of Utaudo municipality—exemplifies the cascading effect of this tragedy. All three women had immobilizing health complications and, unable to evacuate, were killed on Sept. 24 when a mudslide buried the home where they rested.

An American Humanitarian Crisis

If the situation in Puerto Rico seems dire, that's because it is. People on the island will face seemingly insurmountable problems in nearly every aspect of their lives for months to come.

The Trump administration, which has thus far demonstrated a notable lack of concern for the island, could provide some urgent disaster relief by responding Gov. Rosselló's request for increased aid for law enforcement and transportation, among other basic needs.

The U.S. Congress could also play a role in the territory's longer-term recovery. Increasing the island's Medicaid funding, for example, would save lives in this critical time and free up some of the territory's scarce funds for other purposes.

While FEMA picked up the pace of aid five days after the storm, few Puerto Ricans anticipate that they'll see the kind of "historic" federal disaster relief sent to Texas and Florida after hurricanes Harvey and Irma.

Fortunately, Puerto Rico has a culture of resilience. Since the storm, residents have stepped up to help, feed and shelter one another. If the U.S. federal government won't save Puerto Rico, we Puerto Ricans will.

Medical Innovations Have Increased the Well-Being of Millions

Luke Wester

In the following viewpoint, Luke Wester details major medical innovations that gained ground in 2018. Medical innovation is critical to the overall health and wellness of people around the world, as the extension of human life is at the core of every medical breakthrough. With advancements in gene editing technology (CRISPR), medical supply distribution with drones, state-of-the-art vaccines, enhanced post-surgery recovery, an Internet of Things for Healthcare, remote patient monitoring, and advances in diabetes technology, it is more and more likely that these advancements will continue and allow for a better quality of life no matter what level of health. Luke Wester is a content specialist and digital marketing analyst.

As you read, consider the following questions:

1. Which diseases has the FDA approved the use of gene editing, and why?
2. What are three ways in which drone use revolutionizes medical transport?
3. Why is it critical that advancements also come on the recovery side of surgery?

M edical innovations have pushed the envelope of possibility and increased the well-being of millions. This year is no different. Doctors and researchers on the forefront of medicine and technology are enhancing patient care in a number of ways with technology spearheading the initiatives.

The contentment and extension of human life is at the core of every medical breakthrough. These five medical innovations are gaining ground in 2018—some may even see drastic improvements in their application.

Ending Disease with CRISPR Technology

Gene editing technology known as CRISPR is focused on improving the world, one DNA strand at a time. Medical innovations like this aim to improve genetic makeup by removing flaws and awakening dormant traits.

By using a protein called Cas9, scientists are able to separate genetic snippets, which is the first step in altering a DNA structure. CRISPR excels in its ability to identify particular DNA sequences. This allows scientists to clearly identify flawed or malfunctioning DNA segments. The flawed segments can then be removed from DNA, leaving behind a more ideal DNA strand.

Cas9 is assigned an RNA sequence that pairs with the RNA of the flawed DNA portion. This allows Cas9 to locate and inject its RNA into the flawed DNA portion. The following chemical reaction forces a split in the DNA at the flawed portion. In some cases, Cas9 places native and unflawed DNA segments into the section of the DNA where the flaw has been removed in order to get the cell to function properly again.

CRISPR technology has wide-ranging applications, spanning from human gene therapy to agriculture and animals. Diseases like cancer and other inherited ailments can literally be erased from genetics. A main focal point for CRISPR technology is fixing genetic defects, such as retinal disease, in humans.

Before gene editing makes muscles bigger and hair thicker, it will be used only on diseases where researchers have made little headway using other methods. Some retinal diseases have no cure or treatment available on the market, so CRISPR is the only option. Fortunately, the eyes are well-suited for gene editing due to their immuno-related ability.

The FDA approved gene editing for certain retinal diseases in late 2017. Now, the door is open for other gene therapies in allopathic medicine and patients have hope to preserve their ability to see.

Medical Supply Distribution by Drone

Interest in drones spiked years ago when the first affordable and commercially successful drones hit the market. Since then, the global community has come together in an effort to solve some of the world's problems with this new technology.

Agriculture, construction, and cinematography have taken advantage of the opportunities provided by drones. For many people affected by natural disasters, drones helped tremendously. When hurricanes wrecked Puerto Rico, drones were used to survey infrastructure and help restore telecommunication services, allowing people to call for help and receive emergency assistance.

Medical transport has also been revolutionized by drones. The U.S. has been reluctant to allow a drone free-for-all and for good reason. Without strict airspace regulation, drones may do more harm than good. But with proper regulation, drones can help transport medical supplies like blood and medication.

Africa is already seeing a huge benefit from drone-transported medical supplies. Rwanda, a country that has little in the way of roads and no railway system at all, saw great use in medical transport by drone.

The San Francisco-based drone company Zipline transported emergency medical supplies to centers in Rwanda and racked up more than 62,000 flight miles with its drones. The company now has proof of concept and seeks to expand its model to help the neighboring country of Tanzania. The government there has made a partnership with the drone company, transporting medical supplies to remote areas of Tanzania. The move is a major medical innovation for the region and serves as a glimpse of the benefit to come from drones.

State-of-the-Art Vaccines

On average, FDA approved vaccines cost hundreds of millions of dollars and take about a decade to develop. The current approval process for vaccines is not fit for the demands of modern day virus outbreaks and is in need of expedition.

Investors want rapid development of vaccines in order to circumvent the damage caused by pandemics and are looking into the validity of a universal vaccine—think of it like a cure-all for all flu strains.

Vaccine typicity is diversifying too. Egg-based vaccines have been problematic for some due to egg allergies and not idea for cultivation antibody properties, so new types are being developed. Recombinant, and cell-based vaccines are showing promise to improve upon vaccine creation—particularly for their ability for rapid production, making them ideal for pandemic outbreaks.

While researchers are hard at work developing state-of-the-art vaccines, companies are working on new ways to administer the doses. Children and parents cringe when they think of vaccines— mostly because of the pain and discomfort of needle injections. This has prompted companies to evaluate the validity of oral, nasal, and topical patches for inoculation.

Companies are also looking for ways to expand the logistical reach of vaccinations, opting to freeze dry shipments in order to reach remote locations. Will we see drones delivering freeze-dried vaccines on Africa?

Enhanced Recovery After Surgery

Allopathic medicine shines in emergency care and trauma—surgery being a common method of treatment. Inpatient surgeries account for millions of annual hospital visits and the recovery process can be difficult. Problems have risen, not in the act of surgery, but in post-care protocol. Abused prescription medications created an opioid epidemic in the U.S., and many healthcare professionals intend to find better post-surgery recovery practices.

The recovery process has remained relatively unchanged for decades: opiate-based pills to manage pain and bed rest to allow healing. But the paradigm is shifting. Physicians are implementing pain pill alternatives to reduce the risk of addiction and changing the idea of bed rest post surgery. In many cases, light movement such as walking after surgery enhances the healing process; resting in bed was a commonly accepted practice just a few years ago. Nutrition is now intimately involved with the healing process rather than an afterthought.

The benefits of enhanced recovery after surgery affect both patients and hospitals. The goal of every patient is to treat their issue and return to full health, the quicker the better. These new postoperative protocols help patients do just that. One study observed a 33 percent reduction in surgical complications and a decrease of admittance to nursing facilities after surgery. The study also found a reduction in the risk of opiate abuse with the use other analgesic pain management options.

Enhanced recovery after surgery has also helped hospitals save money through decreased readmission rates and through patients spending less time in the hospital. As these new post-surgery protocols become commonplace in 2018, expect to see hospitals saving money and patients experiencing less hassle in the recovery process.

Internet of Things for Healthcare

The Internet of Things, also known as IoT in an interconnected group of smart devices. This has been a hot topic since the emergence of sensor-laden devices created the need for an infrastructure to coordinate them.

Healthcare is a multi-trillion dollar industry with regular improvements from technology. As medical devices continue to advance, so does the need for a system to connect them all. Enter the Internet of Things for Healthcare.

A cloud-connected collection of medical wearables, devices, and sensors allows physicians to monitor the conditions of their patients at an unprecedented level. Troves of data are now available to doctors, enabling them to understand each individual patient's condition on a deeper level and treat them more accurately.

Patients also stand to benefit from the technology, as they also have more access to their own health data, allowing them to make more informed decisions about their own wellness. Collecting personal health data is also fairly simple. Numerous technology companies like Apple offer wearable devices that gather the owners personal sleep, hydration, and exercise data.

But the Internet of Things for Healthcare is seeing a slow evolution, why? The medical infrastructure is enormous and full of strict protocols and procedures. Although simpler things like regular doctor's visit can be enhanced by wearable-collected health data, more serious medical visits have yet to be fully vetted. Things like surgery and in-patient monitoring can be complex and warrant a closer examination before switching from tried and true methods.

Remote Patient Monitoring

Remote patient monitoring is nothing new, but similar to the Medical IoT, technology now offers much more robust data that enhances remote communication between patient and physician.

Smartphones and tablets have connected us in ways like never before. They allow patients to access physicians more easily, at the same time providing physicians more accurate patient health data.

Medical innovations like remote patient monitoring are much needed as the number of physicians are on the decline. People are now looking to expedite the medical process and crystal clear virtual meetings and cloud based medical documents make it possible for doctors to check on their patient from the comfort of their own home or anywhere else for that matter. The market seems to be ready for the change.

The rising costs of healthcare and time commitment of a doctor's visit is becoming obsolete for some instances. A virtual appointment is just as effective and less costly for patients who are refilling certain prescriptions, for example.

Remote patient monitoring also makes it easier for physicians to see more patients. The number of health insurance policies is on the rise, making it challenging for doctors to see and treat the number of patients. RPM allows for quick virtual appointments and patient assessment.

Medical innovations have the power to change millions of lives for the better. With CRISPR, people may regain the precious gift of sight. An untold number of people in Africa will be able to receive medical treatment—for some, it will save their lives. Technology lends a helping hand by making communication, connectivity, and processes better than ever before. These medical innovations set the stage for the future of healthcare and the advancement of medical practices.

Advances in Diabetes Technology

Traditionally, diabetics must painfully prick their finger in order to check blood for glucose levels but new closed-loop insulin delivery systems aim to change all that. The administration of insulin is automated in a closed-loop system, making it easier and less painful for diabetics to maintain healthy blood sugar levels.

The closed-loop system is also known as the artificial pancreas which operates off a monitoring device that controls an insulin pump. The system is customizable and capable of delivering insulin based on the needs of the patient.

Smart pens for insulin injection have also been a big help for diabetic patients. They are more user-friendly than the vial and syringe method but are still easy to carry around with you. Smart pens also offer more accurate insulin doses and better needle protection.

Equipped with smartphone applications and bluetooth connectivity, smart pens can track injection times, insulin units delivered, and additional information with extreme precision. These smart pens are ideal for diabetic patients that have to administer multiple injections a day.

Diabetic patients have a wide range of needs. These diabetic innovations help deliver on the individual needs of each patient. The closed-loop insulin system may work best for some while smart pens may be a better option for others. In any case, managing diabetes has never been more viable than right now.

In Syria the Government Is Attacking Hospitals

Dylan Collins

In the following viewpoint, Dylan Collins interviews Dr. Michele Heisler, a professor at the University of Michigan Medical School and board member of the Physicians for Human Rights (PHR) about the healthcare situation in Syria—specifically, how healthcare workers have endured despite the limited access to equipment, medication, supplies and adequately trained staff. With the Syrian government attacking 95 percent of hospitals in eastern Aleppo, it is impossible for the remaining medical professionals to do their work as normal— providing medical care to the civilians in need. The attacks have forced all medical professionals to work emergency medicine, rather than working in their given specialties. Dylan Collins is an independent journalist based in the Middle East since 2010. His work has appeared in the Guardian *and* Al-Jazeera America.

As you read, consider the following questions:

1. What is the most significant impact of the loss of functioning hospitals in eastern Aleppo and why?
2. Why would a healthcare system be targeted as a weapon of war?
3. Is it possible for aid organizations to fill in the healthcare coverage gaps in Aleppo?

"'Attacks on Aleppo Hospitals are Weapon of War': Q&A," by Dylan Collins, News Deeply, December 1, 2015. Reprinted by permission.

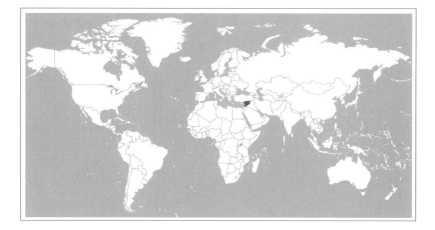

The Syrian government has "decimated" the health care system in eastern Aleppo, according to a report released this month by Physicians for Human Rights (PHR).

In the past three years, the rebel-held half of Syria's northernmost city has suffered 45 direct government attacks on healthcare facilities. More than two-thirds of the area's hospitals no longer function and approximately 95 percent of doctors have fled, been killed or detained, according to the report. The assortment of doctors and nurses that remain—roughly 60 to 80 doctors and 200 nurses that work on a rotating basis—are forced to work jobs far afield from their original area of expertise.

During a two-week period in July 2015, PHR researchers interviewed 24 physicians and other health professions working in the 10 remaining hospitals—there were 33 functioning in 2010—in eastern Aleppo.

Entitled, *Aleppo Abandoned: A Case Study on Health Care in Syria*, the report details how healthcare workers have managed despite limited access to equipment, medication, supplies and trained staff.

"The Syrian government is using attacks on Aleppo's healthcare system as a weapon of war," said Dr. Michele Heisler, a professor at the University of Michigan Medical School, a PHR board member and one of the report's investigators. "The systematic targeting of hospitals is the biggest impediment to providing healthcare in Syria. The physicians I met want one thing—for the bombing to stop so they can do their work."

Syria Deeply spoke with Heisler shortly after the report was published to find out PHR's methodology and the current state of affairs for health providers in eastern Aleppo.

Syria Deeply: One of the headlines of the report states that in eastern Aleppo less than a third of the hospitals are functioning, 95 percent of the doctors have fled, been detained or have been killed, so who is left to run the healthcare system there?

Dr. Michel Heisler: There is a core of pretty phenomenal physicians and other health professionals maintaining services in the area. As you can imagine—although if you look at the whole report, I think the largest hospital at any one time has about 13 physicians—a lot of the medical care has been task-shifted. And you can imagine although if you look at the whole report, I think the largest hospital at any one time has about 13 physicians, but a lot of the medical care has been task-shifted. They've been remarkably resilient. There are still three functioning dialysis units in eastern Aleppo, but there are absolutely no kidney doctors, so all of the dialysis units are staffed by technicians and they've worked out very ingenious ways of making the best of what they have in terms of equipment.

There is a very small core of surgeons and physicians. Almost all of the physicians we spoke to had been pediatricians, and are now basically working in emergency medicine, actually doing residencies to learn how to do surgery. You have people that are trained in one field having to learn on the job how to provide care in another field ... You have general surgeons working as vascular surgeons—there's a terrible scarcity of vascular surgeons. As one physician said: "We're able to save lives but many legs are being amputated that wouldn't have to be if we had more vascular surgeons." There are currently no functioning CT scans or MRIs in the city, so that's especially problematic. As you can imagine, with all the barrel bombs and the air attacks, a lot of people are incurring traumatic brain injuries. Without a CT scan or an MRI, you really can't do brain surgery. We actually have some neurosurgeons in the city but you really can't … a lot of people are dying because they can't image the brain, and without the imaging, they can't really go in and figure out how to help them.

So it's a lot of improvisation, and an unbelievable amount heroism, certainly. A lot of the doctors we spoke to, all of their families are already in Germany or in Europe. Their families are begging them to leave Aleppo. Many of the physicians have transferred their families to Gaziantep or other places in southern Turkey. The physicians basically go to Aleppo for 15 to 20 days, they stay at the hospital in part because it's too dangerous to go back and forth with the barrel bombs, so they kind of work 24/7 for 15 to 20 days, and then they go and just collapse and rest in Turkey. They realize that they really need to give themselves periods of rest otherwise they'll get burnt out, they'll get demoralized—and actually one physician said that, without the breaks, they become less empathetic doctors.

They are just very matter of fact. The humility is remarkable. I mean, everyone we talk to, we're all like, "Wow how can you do this?," and they're like, "How can I not do this? I'm a doctor and this is my city." There are still about 400,000 civilians in eastern Aleppo. As one ophthalmologist said: "You know, if I leave, if someone has a foreign object in their eye, they wont have anyone to help them." And they're aware in the midst of barrel bombs, there are not going to be new physicians coming. So basically this is the group of doctors that is trying to hold steady to provide medical care.

Syria Deeply: How have national and international aid organizations helped to fill the gaps in coverage when it comes to supplies and personnel?

Dr. Michel Heisler: We went into this thinking they're going to talk about shortages and lack of medicine, but pretty much all the physicians said the first and the last thing they need is safety. As one physician said: If you can't protect your staff, if the hospitals are being bombed, then it doesn't matter if you have medicine.

Syria Deeply: Who is responsible for targeting these medical facilities in the eastern area of the city?

Dr. Michel Heisler: The Syrian government has hit over 95 percent of them. And again, they have airplanes so the air strikes are coming from the Syrian government. They are systematic attacks, certainly some of them are deliberate attacks, certainly some of them also with barrel bombs. You know if they drop a bomb on a school or a mosque or a civilian structure then there are times that the hospital is affected by the blast. PHR has adopted a very rigorous methodology requiring corroboration from different independent sources. I think at the very beginning of our interviews, PHR thought maybe these strikes are all a result of collateral damage. However, a couple of things argue against that. First, most of the major hospitals stand alone. They're not near any buildings that could be a legitimate military target. I will also emphasize the hospitals are still in the same place as they've always been. It would kind of be like our government not knowing where Mass General is. They very much have started trying to move their procedures and operations into the basements to protect themselves from the bombs. They've tried to keep the lights off to protect themselves from the bombs. PHR also obtained satellite imagery of just before the attack and just after the attack, and that allowed for it to rule out claims that there may have been a legitimate military target in the vicinity at the time. Again, these hospitals are all in the city, they are not on the front lines. These are in civilian areas.

There are very compelling reasons to believe that both doctors and hospitals are being targeted, and that this is being used as a weapon of war to terrorize civilians. And, I'm sure, to deplete civilians living in eastern Aleppo. The other circumstantial evidence is that many of the hospitals have been hit more than once.

Syria Deeply: You were quoted as saying that the Syrian government is using the attacks against Aleppo's health care system as a weapon of war.

Dr. Michel Heisler: One of the points that we're trying to really get across is that unfortunately, and as tragic as this is the case, a lot of people chalk it up to chaos and collateral damage. If there is not mobilization against this in the way that there was mobilization against the Syrian government's use of sarin gas against its own civilians in 2013, then this will become a standard weapon of war. It is an insidiously effective weapon—to sow fear. I mean, you're attacking safe spaces where wounded people and ill people are going to be healed, and where people have made an oath to heal them. When these places are directly targeted—that's a devastatingly effective weapon of war.

Periodical and Internet Sources Bibliography

The following articles have been selected to supplement the diverse views presented in this chapter.

Nicole Acevedo, "Puerto Rico has gotten far less aid than Trump has claimed, report shows," NBC News, May 14, 2019. https://www.nbcnews.com/news/latino/puerto-rico-has-gotten-far-less-aid-trump-has-claimed-n1005506.

Africa Science News, "Strengthening health systems to better fight infectious diseases in Africa," Africa Science News, May 12, 2019. http://africasciencenews.org/strengthening-health-systems-to-better-fight-infectious-diseases-in-africa/.

Nyka Alexander, "WHO public health advice regarding the Olympics and Zika virus," World Health Organization, May 28, 2016. https://www.who.int/news-room/detail/28-05-2016-who-public-health-advice-regarding-the-olympics-and-zika-virus.

Amir Attaran, "Zika virus and the 2016 Olympic Games," *Lancet*, July 22, 2016. https://www.thelancet.com/journals/laninf/article/PIIS1473-3099(16)30230-4/fulltext.

Editorial, "First confirmed AIDS death in U.S. was 50 years ago today," *Roanoke Times*, May 14, 2019. https://www.roanoke.com/opinion/editorials/editorial-first-confirmed-aids-death-in-u-s-was-years/article_878a7be9-30a0-5ba2-b9df-d0c65358fd45.html.

Yessenia Funes, "Hurricane Maria Left Thousands of Puerto Rican Children Experiencing Symptoms of PTSD, Survey Finds," Gizmodo, May 1, 2019. https://earther.gizmodo.com/hurricane-maria-left-thousands-of-puerto-rican-children-1834450309.

Sujata Gupta, "Facebook data show how many people left Puerto Rico after Hurricane Maria," Science News, May 3, 2019. https://www.sciencenews.org/article/facebook-data-show-how-many-people-left-puerto-rico-after-hurricane-maria.

Erin Murray, "Puerto Rican Family Moves Into Abandoned School After Hurricane Maria," Spectrum News 13, May 13, 2019.

https://www.mynews13.com/fl/orlando/news/2019/05/13/puerto-rican-family-forced-to-move-into-school-after-hurricane-maria.

Newroom, "Cleveland Clinic Unveils Top 10 Medical Innovations for 2018," Newsroom, October 25, 2017. https://newsroom. clevelandclinic.org/2017/10/25/cleveland-clinic-unveils-top-10-medical-innovations-for-2018/.

Carly Olson, "A New Marc Quinn Art Installation Spotlights the Global Refugee Crisis," *Architectural Digest*, April 23, 2019. https://www.architecturaldigest.com/story/new-marc-quinn-art-installation-spotlights-global-refugee-crisis.

Philippa Stroud, "Turkey's strategy for dealing with the Syrian refugee crisis is an example to Europe," *Times*, May 2, 2019. https://www. thetimes.co.uk/article/syria-refugee-crisis-turkey-displaced-aid-strategy-cw00srvtv.

UNAIDS, "Keeping up the momentum in the global AIDS response," UNAIDS, April 24, 2019. https://www.unaids.org/en/resources/ presscentre/featurestories/2019/april/20190424_southafrica.

Ford Vox, "What real threat does Zika pose to the Rio Olympics? History has an answer," CNN, February 12, 2016. https://www. cnn.com/2016/02/12/health/zika-olympics-threat/index.html.

CHAPTER 2

What Impact Does Fake News Have on Global Health?

The "Seminal" Article Linking the MMR Vaccine and Autism Was Fraudulent

Fiona Godlee, Jane Smith, and Harvey Marcovitch

In the following viewpoint, Fiona Godlee, Jane Smith, and Harvey Marcovitch recap the fraudulent paper published by Andrew Wakefield and 12 others in 1998, which allegedly linked the measles, mumps, and rubella (MMR) vaccine to autism and bowel disease. In the decades that followed, epidemiological studies consistently found that there was no link between the MMR vaccine and autism, but despite that, this inaccurate stigma has persisted. In 2004, ten of the coauthors of Wakefield's paper came together and retracted the paper's interpretation, but Wakefield refused to, even though he had opportunities to replicate his findings or admit he was mistaken. Fiona Godlee is editor in chief for the BMJ. *Jane Smith is deputy editor for the* BMJ. *Harvey Marcovitch is associate editor for the* BMJ.

As you read, consider the following questions:

1. What were the conflicts of interest leading to the realization that Wakefield's research was likely unfounded?
2. What is the Office of Research Integrity and how does it define fraud?
3. How does this fraudulent paper inform the veracity of the rest of Wakefield's research?

"Wakefield's Article Linking MMR Vaccine and Autism Was Fraudulent," by Fiona Godlee, Jane Smith and Harvey Marcovitch, BMJ Publishing Group, January 6, 2011. Reprinted by permission.

S cience is at once the most questioning and ... sceptical of
activities and also the most trusting," said Arnold Relman,
former editor of the New England Journal of Medicine, in 1989.
"It is intensely sceptical about the possibility of error, but totally
trusting about the possibility of fraud."[1] Never has this been
truer than of the 1998 *Lancet* paper that implied a link between
the measles, mumps, and rubella (MMR) vaccine and a "new
syndrome" of autism and bowel disease.

Authored by Andrew Wakefield and 12 others, the paper's
scientific limitations were clear when it appeared in 1998.[2,3] As
the ensuing vaccine scare took off, critics quickly pointed out that
the paper was a small case series with no controls, linked three
common conditions, and relied on parental recall and beliefs.[4] Over
the following decade, epidemiological studies consistently found no
evidence of a link between the MMR vaccine and autism.[5, 6, 7, 8] By
the time the paper was finally retracted 12 years later,[9] after forensic
dissection at the General Medical Council's (GMC) longest ever
fitness to practise hearing,[10] few people could deny that it was fatally
flawed both scientifically and ethically. But it has taken the diligent
scepticism of one man, standing outside medicine and science, to
show that the paper was in fact an elaborate fraud.

In a series of articles starting this week, and seven years after
first looking into the MMR scare, journalist Brian Deer now
shows the extent of Wakefield's fraud and how it was perpetrated
(doi:10.1136/bmj.c5347). Drawing on interviews, documents, and
data made public at the GMC hearings, Deer shows how Wakefield
altered numerous facts about the patients' medical histories in order
to support his claim to have identified a new syndrome; how his
institution, the Royal Free Hospital and Medical School in London,
supported him as he sought to exploit the ensuing MMR scare for
financial gain; and how key players failed to investigate thoroughly
in the public interest when Deer first raised his concerns.[11]

Deer published his first investigation into Wakefield's paper in
2004.[12] This uncovered the possibility of research fraud, unethical
treatment of children, and Wakefield's conflict of interest through

Measles Outbreaks

The coverage rate for the measles, mumps and rubella (MMR) vaccine in San Antonio is 93 percent, which means about 6,000 children in Bexar County have not received their shots. It's not clear why. It's possible some parents don't have the proper knowledge or access to care, Mangla said.

But some parents choose not to vaccinate their children against preventable contagious diseases, often because they fear damaging effects of the shots.

Stay-at-home mother Kelli Hicks is one of them. She has no plans to vaccinate her daughter against measles—or anything else. She believes the risk of harm from the shots outweighs the risk of measles, she said.

"I don't want to play Russian roulette with my baby," said Hicks, 23, who researched vaccines during the nine months she was pregnant with Kali Jo, now 4 months old. "I don't feel the need to pump my child full of toxins."

In January, 102 people from 14 states were reported to have measles, more than 90 percent of them part of an outbreak traced to Disneyland. Most people who contracted the disease weren't vaccinated against it, the Centers for Disease Control and Prevention reports.

Most people in the U.S. have been vaccinated against measles. Still, the disease pops up in the U.S. when unvaccinated travelers, either American

his involvement with a lawsuit against manufacturers of the MMR vaccine. Building on these findings, the GMC launched its own proceedings that focused on whether the research was ethical. But while the disciplinary panel was examining the children's medical records in public, Deer compared them with what was published in the Lancet. His focus was now on whether the research was true.

The Office of Research Integrity in the United States defines fraud as fabrication, falsification, or plagiarism.[13] Deer unearthed clear evidence of falsification. He found that not one of the[12] cases reported in the 1998 Lancet paper was free of misrepresentation or undisclosed alteration, and that in no single case could the medical records be fully reconciled with the descriptions, diagnoses, or histories published in the journal.

citizens or foreign visitors, contract it in another country and spread it to people who are not protected from it, said Dr. George Crawford, professor of medicine and infectious diseases at the University of Texas Health Science Center.

Public health officials say that lack of vaccination could contribute to the re-emergence of preventable diseases once declared eliminated in the U.S.

Last year, the U.S. had 644 reports of people with measles, the highest since the disease was declared eliminated in 2000. The CDC blames higher numbers of cases in recent years on increased cases in some countries, such as the Philippines, to which Americans often travel and to the spread of the disease among pockets of unvaccinated people.

"The data clearly indicate that lower immunization rates contribute to increased rates of secondary transmission," said Dr. Bryan Alsip, chief medical officer at University Health System.

Still, the choice of parents not to vaccinate their children "is probably less common than people would think," Alsip said. "I think there are clusters and groups probably scattered in various parts of the country."

"Lack of Vaccinations Linked to Measles Outbreak," by San Antonio Express News, Jessica Belasco, February 3, 2015.

Who perpetrated this fraud? There is no doubt that it was Wakefield. Is it possible that he was wrong, but not dishonest: that he was so incompetent that he was unable to fairly describe the project, or to report even one of the 12 children's cases accurately? No. A great deal of thought and effort must have gone into drafting the paper to achieve the results he wanted: the discrepancies all led in one direction; misreporting was gross. Moreover, although the scale of the GMC's 217 day hearing precluded additional charges focused directly on the fraud, the panel found him guilty of dishonesty concerning the study's admissions criteria, its funding by the Legal Aid Board, and his statements about it afterwards.[14]

Furthermore, Wakefield has been given ample opportunity either to replicate the paper's findings, or to say he was mistaken. He

He has declined to do either. He refused to join 10 of his coauthors in retracting the paper's interpretation in 2004,[15] and has repeatedly denied doing anything wrong at all. Instead, although now disgraced and stripped of his clinical and academic credentials, he continues to push his views.[16]

Meanwhile the damage to public health continues, fuelled by unbalanced media reporting and an ineffective response from government, researchers, journals, and the medical profession.[17,18] Although vaccination rates in the United Kingdom have recovered slightly from their 80% low in 2003-4,[19] they are still below the 95% level recommended by the World Health Organization to ensure herd immunity. In 2008, for the first time in 14 years, measles was declared endemic in England and Wales.[20] Hundreds of thousands of children in the UK are currently unprotected as a result of the scare, and the battle to restore parents' trust in the vaccine is ongoing.

Any effect of the scare on the incidence of mumps remains in question. In epidemics in the UK, the US, and the Netherlands, peak prevalence was in 18-24 year olds, of whom 70-88% had been immunised with at least one dose of the MMR vaccine.[21,22] Any consequence of a fall in uptake after 1998 may not become apparent until the cohorts of children affected reach adolescence. One clue comes from an outbreak in a school in Essen, Germany, attended by children whose parents were opposed to vaccinations. Of the 71 children infected with mumps, 68 had not been immunised.[23]

But perhaps as important as the scare's effect on infectious disease is the energy, emotion, and money that have been diverted away from efforts to understand the real causes of autism and how to help children and families who live with it.[24]

There are hard lessons for many in this highly damaging saga. Firstly, for the coauthors. The GMC panel was clear that it was Wakefield alone who wrote the final version of the paper. His coauthors seem to have been unaware of what he was doing under the cover of their names and reputations. As the GMC panel heard, they did not even know which child was which in the paper's patient anonymised text and tables. However, this does not absolve them. Although only two (John Walker-Smith and Simon Murch) were charged by the GMC, and only one, the paper's senior author Walker-Smith, was found guilty of misconduct, they all failed in their duties as authors. The satisfaction of adding to one's CV must never detract from the responsibility to ensure that one has been neither party to nor duped by a fraud. This means that coauthors will have to check the source data of studies more thoroughly than many do at present—or alternatively describe in a contributor's statement precisely which bits of the source data they take responsibility for.

Secondly, research ethics committees should not only scrutinise proposals but have systems to check that what is done is what was permitted (with an audit trail for any changes) and work to a governance procedure that can impose sanctions where an eventual publication proves this was not the case. Finally, there are lessons for the Royal Free Hospital, the Lancet, and the wider scientific community. These will be considered in forthcoming articles.

What of Wakefield's other publications? In light of this new information their veracity must be questioned. Past experience tells us that research misconduct is rarely isolated behaviour.[25] Over the years, the BMJ and its sister journals Gut and Archives of Disease in Childhood have published a number of articles, including letters and abstracts, by Wakefield and colleagues. We have written to the vice provost of UCL, John Tooke, who now has responsibility for Wakefield's former institution, to ask for an investigation into all of his work to decide whether any more papers should be retracted.

The *Lancet* paper has of course been retracted, but for far narrower misconduct than is now apparent. The retraction statement cites the GMC's findings that the patients were not consecutively referred and the study did not have ethical approval, leaving the door open for those who want to continue to believe that the science, flawed though it always was, still stands. We hope that declaring the paper a fraud will close that door for good.

References

1. Schechter AN, Wyngaarden JB, Edsall JT, Maddox J, Relman AS, Angell M, et al. Colloquium on scientific authorship: rights and responsibilities. FASEB J1989;3:209-17.

2. Wakefield AJ, Murch SH, Anthony A, Linnell, Casson DM, Malik M, et al. Ileal lymphoid nodular hyperplasia, non-specific colitis, and pervasive developmental disorder in children [retracted]. Lancet1998;351:637-41.

3. Chen RT, DeStefano F. Vaccine adverse events: causal or coincidental? Lancet 1998;351:611-2.

4. Payne C, Mason B. Autism, inflammatory bowel disease, and MMR vaccine. Lancet1998;351:907.

5. Black C, Kaye JA, Jick H. Relation of childhood gastrointestinal disorders to autism: nested casecontrol study using data from the UK General Practice Research Database. BMJ2002;325:419-21.

6. Taylor B, Miller E, Lingam R, Andrews N, Simmons A, Stowe J. Measles, mumps, and rubella vaccination and bowel problems or developmental regression in children with autism: population study. BMJ2002;324:393-6.

7. Madsen KM, Hviid A, Vestergaard M, Schendel D, Wohlfahrt J, Thorsen P, et al. A population-based study of measles, mumps, and rubella vaccination and autism. N Engl J Med2002;347:1477-82.

8. Honda H, Shimizu Y, Rutter M. No effect of MMR withdrawal on the incidence of autism: a total population study. J Child Psychol Psychiatry2005;46:572-9.

9. The editors of the Lancet. Retraction—Ileal-lymphoid-nodular hyperplasia, non-specific colitis, and pervasive developmental disorder in children. Lancet2010;375:445.

10. Transcripts of hearings of fitness to practise panel (misconduct) in the case of Wakefield, Walker-Smith, and Murch, 16 July 2007 to 24 May 2010. GMC; 2010.

11. Deer B. Secrets of the MMR scare: how the case against the MMR vaccine was fixed. BMJ2011;342:c5347.

12. Deer B. Revealed: MMR research scandal. Sunday Times2004 February 22. www.timesonline.co.uk/tol/life_and_style/health/article1027636.ece.

13. Office of Research Integrity. Definition of research misconduct. http://ori.hhs.gov/misconduct/definition_misconduct.shtml.

14. GMC. Andrew Wakefield: determination of serious professional misconduct 24 May 2010. www.gmc-uk.org/Wakefield_SPM_and_SANCTION.pdf_32595267.pdf.

15. Murch SH, Anthony A, Casson DH, Malik M, Berelowitz M, Dhillon AP, et al. Retraction of an interpretation. Lancet2004;363:750.

16. Shenoy R. Controversial autism researcher tells local Somalis disease is solvable. Minnesota Public Radio2010 December 17. http://minnesota.publicradio.org/display/web/2010/12/17/somali-autism.

17. Hilton S, Hunt K, Langan M, Hamilton V, Petticrew M. Reporting of MMR evidence in professional publications: 1988–2007. Arch Dis Child2009;94:831-3.

18. Bedford HE, Elliman DAC. MMR vaccine and autism. BMJ2010 Feb 2;340:c655.

19. Health Protection Agency. Completed primary course at two years of age: England and Wales, 1966-1977, England only 1978 onwards. http://www.hpa.org.uk/web/HPAweb&HPAwebStandard/HPAweb_C/1195733819251.

20. Health Protection Agency. Confirmed cases of measles, mumps and rubella 1996-2009. http://www.hpa.org.uk/web/HPAweb&HPAwebStandard/HPAweb_C/1195733833790.

21. Jick H, Chamberlin DP, Hagberg KW. The origin and spread of a mumps epidemic: United Kingdom, 2003-2006. Epidemiology2009;20:656-61.

22. Kutty PK, Kruszon-Moran DM, Dayan GH, Alexander JP, Williams NJ, Garcia PE, et al. Seroprevalence of antibody to mumps virus in the US population, 1999-2004. J Infect Dis2010;202:667-74.

23. Roggendorf H, Mankertz A, Kundt R, Roggendorf M. Spotlight on measles 2010: measles outbreak in a mainly unvaccinated community in Essen, Germany, March-June 2010. Euro Surveill2010;15:2. http://www.eurosurveillance.org/ViewArticle.aspx?ArticleId=19605.

24. Oakley GP, Johnstone RB. Balancing the benefits and harms in public health prevention programmes mandated by governments. BMJ2004;329:41-3.

25. Rennie D. Misconduct and journal peer review. In: Godlee F, Jefferson T eds. Peer Review in Health Sciences, 2nd ed. BMJ Books; 2003. p 118-129.]

Why Patients Turn to Celebrities for Medical Advice

Brad Sopher

In the following viewpoint, Brad Sopher details how and why celebrities have such an impact on medical decisions. With Facebook posts going viral in any and all topics, medical advice is not spared—and that allows people to very likely discover inaccurate information about their ailments. The "celebrity effect" can be seen in recent years, including in 2013 when Angelina Jolie revealed her decision to undergo a bilateral prophylactic mastectomy, because of the very specific genetic predisposition she has for developing breast cancer. While bringing awareness to breast cancer and genetic testing was a benefit to Jolie's story, what gets lost in the stories are the specific details of how her genetic predisposition are not the standard in the breast cancer community. Brad Sopher is vice president and co-founder at Rendia.

As you read, consider the following questions:

1. What examples, if any, show the benefits to people following medical advice from celebrities?
2. How does celebrity influence pose a negative impact on public perception of health decisions?
3. What are the ways doctors can mitigate the influence of celebrities in the medical field?

D o you think your patients are too smart to be influenced by health advice from celebrities? There's no way educated adults would make medical decisions based on a viral Facebook post or an article about a movie star in the news, right? That's what Valerie A. Jones, M.D., thought, too, until she Googled the HPV vaccine, curious to see what her patients might find. "I was disgusted, angry, and even saddened by what I found," she wrote on KevinMD.com, describing the sensationalized, medically inaccurate stories that filled her search results.

Whether it's well-meaning celebrities trying to increase awareness, such as actress Angelina Jolie sharing her decision to have a preventive mastectomy, or downright dangerous misinformation, such as the anti-vaccine stances of celebrities including Jenny McCarthy, here's why your patients listen to health advice from famous people, and what you can do about it.

Data Show Influence of Celebrities' Health Stories on Public

Before her Google experience, Dr. Jones said she was "blissfully unaware of the public's perception" of medical treatment recommendations. "I ignorantly assumed most people go to their physician first for medical information."

Numerous studies published in medical journals show that the public is, in fact, measurably influenced by celebrity health stories. A study published last year examined the "celebrity effect" on medical choices by looking at the example of Angelina Jolie's public decision to undergo a bilateral prophylactic mastectomy in 2013 after learning she had a genetic predisposition for developing breast cancer.

"The researchers found the rate of risk-reducing mastectomies spiked after Jolie's announcement that she'd undergone the procedure," with a 50 percent increase in the geographic regions examined during a one-year period, reported NBC News.

CNN reported that after actor Charlie Sheen announced that he was HIV-positive in 2015, sales of in-home HIV testing kits

"Vaccine Hesitancy" Could Be Deadly

The development has sparked concerns that parents deliberately choosing not to vaccinate their children—out of scientifically unfounded concerns that vaccinations can harm them—are leading to epidemics that could easily be avoided.

Washington governor Jay Inslee recently declared a state of emergency in response to a growing number of measles cases in the city of Vancouver, which lies within Clark county in the south of the state.

By 29 January, Clark county public health identified 36 confirmed cases of measles and 12 suspected cases. Twenty-five cases involved children under 10, 32 of those affected had not been immunized, and the remaining four had an unconfirmed vaccination status.

CCPH also listed a range of exposure sites including schools, health centers and restaurants. Prominent among the sites were a number of Vancouver-area evangelical churches and Christian academies.

Across the Columbia River in Portland, Oregon, one confirmed case had been identified by 29 January. Exposure sites there included a church; the Moda Center, where the Portland Trailblazers play NBA games; and the Oregon Museum of Science and Industry, an attraction which is popular with the city's children. Another case has been confirmed in King county, which contains Seattle.

reached record highs, according to a study published in *Prevention Science* last year.

What Celebrities Have That Doctors Don't

But why would people listen to celebrities who have no medical training? To science-minded doctors, this may make no sense. "What they do have is a platform, something most doctors and scientists don't have and few will ever possess. People listen to performers with platforms," wrote Nina Shapiro, M.D., director of pediatric otolaryngology at the David Geffen School of Medicine at UCLA and author of Hype: A Doctor's Guide to Medical Myths, Exaggerated Claims and Bad Advice.

Clark county vaccination rates among children are low, and far below what they were in previous decades. Between the 2004-2005 school year and 2017-2018, vaccination rates among Clark county kindergartners fell from 91.4% to 76.5%.

State laws in Oregon and Washington require students who attend schools, or engage with other institutions beyond their home to be vaccinated against a range of diseases. But, unlike in other states, where parents can ask for exemptions on medical grounds, in Oregon and Washington parents can ask for exemptions on religious or philosophical grounds relatively easily.

They do so in significant numbers. According to the CDC, in Oregon 7.5% of kindergartners had non-medical exemptions from vaccinations in 2018. In Washington, it was 3.9%.

Dawn Nolt, an assistant professor of pediatric diseases at Doernbecher children's hospital in Portland, said that while measles is only rarely deadly, "it has high consequences" for the short-term health of its victims. She said measles is also highly contagious, and will spread to 90% of unvaccinated people who are exposed to a carrier of the disease.

She has seen an increase in what practitioners call "vaccine hesitancy", and she added: "I do wonder whether the advent of social media has empowered that anti-vaccine movement."

"Measles Outbreak Sparks Concerns Over Anti-Vaccination Movement," by Jason Wilson, Guardian News and Media Limited, February 2, 2019.

Social scientist Dr. Frank Niles attributes the public's behavior to the "halo effect," at least in the case of Jolie. "When we get exposed to folks through the media we start developing a familiarity almost like they're part of our family," he told NBC News. "When we develop positive associations, anything those celebrities endorse or talk about benefits from the halo effect, meaning when we have positive emotional resonances with that individual, we have similarly positive responses to most anything they do."

Why Celebrities May Do More Harm Than Good

So what's the problem if celebrities shed light on health risks and encourage people to take action? Jolie did do some good by bringing awareness to breast cancer and genetic testing, said doctors interviewed by NBC News. However, the larger and more emotional a story becomes – often the case with celebrity health scares—the more likely it is that nuances will be lost and misinformation will spread.

For instance, breast cancer surgeon Dennis Holmes, M.D., emphasized that Jolie had "a very specific medical diagnosis—a hereditary gene mutation that causes breast cancer—that does not affect the majority of the population, or even the majority of women with breast cancer." He added that mastectomy offers no survival benefit over lumpectomy and radiation.

Some celebrities are doing more serious harm when it comes to vaccines. Jenny McCarthy, a former television host who has linked her son's autism to his vaccination, as well as actresses Mayim Bialik and Alicia Silverstone, have spoken out about not vaccinating their children, often citing a vaccine-autism link stemming from a widely discredited study in the late 1990's.

Think these stories don't influence the public's behavior? The *New York Times* reported that the U.S. is seeing cases of infectious diseases that were thought to be eradicated, including whooping cough and an outbreak of measles at Disneyland in 2015, due in part to the misinformation being circulated by celebrities.

What Doctors Can Do to Minimize Celebrities' Influence on Patients

So what can doctors do to combat this alarming trend? Instead of being reactive, be proactive. Provide patient education in a format that's accessible, appealing, easy to understand, and – this is key—shareable online. Most patients probably won't pass along a brochure, but they might send a link of an informative video to friends or share a blog post on Facebook. For example, this short, simple video explains how vaccines work: https://get.rendia.com/how-it-works/distinguish-your-practice/video10.html.

This post weaves celebrity news into a reader-friendly post about glaucoma, which includes patient education videos: Six

Ways to Improve Glaucoma Awareness (https://blog.rendia.com/ glaucoma_awareness/). And here's an example of how the Harvard Health Blog responded to news reports that *Hamilton* creator Lin-Manuel Miranda has shingles (https://www.health.harvard.edu/ blog/celebrities-get-shingles-too-2018041113632).

Also, doctors need to take an active role in social media, said Dr. Jones. If you never make time to check out Twitter, Facebook, or Instagram, you may not be prepared when patients bring up current issues that are trending online.

She encourages doctors to share medical information in blog posts and on social media. "This is our responsibility. Of course, the public is going to be drawn more to stories of human interest regarding vaccines and latest trends instead of dry, data-heavy medical journals … We need to tell our stories, of course in a HIPAA-compliant way, but tell them in a way people will want to listen or read them."

In Pakistan Polio Is on the Rise Thanks to Attacks on Immunization

Shazia Ghafoor and Nadeem Sheikh

In the following excerpted viewpoint, Shazia Ghafoor and Nadeem Sheikh detail the re-emergence of the poliomyelitis (polio) virus, specifically in Pakistan, Afghanistan, and Nigeria. While the World Health Organization (WHO) has had success in reducing the number of countries impacted by polio from 125 to just the three in the Middle East, those countries have not been able to properly eradicate the disease. A disease that can lead to paralysis, mostly in children under age five, polio can lead to death as the respiratory muscles are paralyzed. While the number of polio cases was at zero in 2007, there was a resurgence in cases a year later. Shazia Ghafoor is pursuing a MPhil in the Department of Zoology, University of the Punjab. Nadeem Sheikh is working as an assistant professor in the department.

As you read, consider the following questions:

1. Why is the polio eradication imitative failing in Pakistan?
2. How is parental perception a critical factor toward stopping the spread of polio in the Middle East?
3. In what ways can the polio eradication in India inform eradication policies in other South Asian countries?

"Eradication and Current Status of Poliomyelitis in Pakistan: Ground Realities," by Shazia Ghafoor and Nadeem Sheikh, Hindawi Publishing Corporation, June 23, 2016. https://www.hindawi.com/journals/jir/2016/6837824/. Licensed under CC BY 4.0 International.

Poliomyelitis (family Picornaviridae), frequently abbreviated as "Polio," is among the most feared viruses of the twentieth century in the world that resulted in commencement of global initiative programme for the eradication of polio by WHO in 1988. Polio being a positively stranded RNA enterovirus is well-known for its ability to affect a part of spinal cord (gray matter), leading to irreversible acute flaccid paralysis (AFP) mostly in children under five due to affected motor neurons, or can result in death if muscles of respiration or throat gets paralyzed but fortunately that is not quite often.[1]

[...]

The most heard GPEI (global polio eradication initiative) launched by WHO 27 years ago has achieved remarkable success in reducing the number of endemic countries from 125 across the globe to only 3 including Pakistan, Afghanistan, and Nigeria, where WPV (wild polio virus) transmission has not yet been interrupted although numerical digit of cases has dropped down by 99% in comparison to 350,000 new cases per annum then (1988).[6-8] Eradication programme has faced much more operational problems in these countries in comparison to the rest of the world.[9-13] World Health Assembly (WHA) has declared the crippling polio disease as PHEIC (Global Public Health Emergency of International Concern) in May 2014.[14]

Polio is among the few strenuous challenges that Pakistan is facing today. Expanded Programme on Immunization (EPI) embarked on the health scenario in 1978 with its fundamental objective to vaccinate children against fatal diseases in their infancy. Polio eradication programme started officially in 1994. NIDs (National Immunization Days) and surveillance resulted in decreasing number of cases markedly to double figure of just 28 in 2005 from 1155 recorded in 1997.[15] WHO has imposed mandatory vaccination for people traveling internationally from Pakistan which has maligned the image of country along with panic and stress among travelers.[16] Polio eradication is the question of life and death for Pakistan. In spite of all efforts, polio is still endemic in Pakistan.

[…]

Why Polio Eradication Initiative Is Failing in Pakistan? Real Scenario behind the Curtain

War Against Terrorism

War against terrorism has badly affected FATA and KPK regions of the country that had been invaded by stateless characters. The puzzle becomes trickier as literacy rate among females is hardly 3%. Since 2004 these areas have been targeted by drone attacks that lead to mass killings (1900–2900 people). Some parts of FATA remained unattended by polio campaign for 3 years due to security concerns and rumors against immunization. As per reported by WHO, in 2011, a major proportion of population, almost 38% children, remained unapproachable for polio vaccination in Khyber Agency, a part of FATA, although the percentage in the next year (2012) was declined to 20%.[23] Further, local religious personalities with their disliking point of view for polio vaccination and workers have substantially affected eradication process.[26]

Life Threatening Attacks against Polio Frontline Workers

Life threatening attacks against polio vaccinators in Pakistan[25] and Nigeria is a way adopted by fanatic groups to seek global attention due to sensitivity of the issue.[27] In a country where almost 40 vaccinators have been killed in such attacks since July 2012, polio surge is not a surprising outcome there. Such attacks result in temporary cessation of the campaign. Having Polio vaccinators and workers often back on duty after a short break of just few weeks is really commendable.[28] Since June 2012, regional tribal leaders of North Waziristan Agency (a part of FATA) have prohibited polio immunization. The Independent Monitoring Board (IMB) reported in February 2014 that health officials responded slowly in grasping basic seriousness of the situation. Such kind of attitude by the officials may result in a situation where Pakistan would be the last endemic country over the globe. It has become mandatory to punish the responsible office bearer in this situation and flawless security needs to be provided to the frontline polio workers in order to revive the campaign to eradicate polio in the affected areas.[29] Aid and immunization are often linked with foreign interests in Pakistan[30] which make all the exercise questionable and debatable at national level. LHVs have been targeted in Swat region for being working for such campaigns and fostering contraceptives[31] for betterment of the women in Pakistan.

Crummy Healthcare Systems

Malpractices in service delivery and loopholes in prevailing health systems are emerging as troublesome matters.[23] Poor healthcare system seems to be a major hurdle in immunization coverage.[32-34] RI (Routine Immunization) rate is low.[35] Flaws in health system allow bundles of corruption both financially and morally resulting in stealing of resources. Absence of staff from duty, lack of field operations, and even use of vaccines for privately run clinics affect service delivery in terms of quantity and quality. Free services (syringes and vaccination cards) are charged. Open vial policy is often misused for personal benefits. Delivery infrastructure through which polio eradication initiative is implemented is underfinanced.[34] Shah et al. (2011) have reported that substandard performance of EPI, insufficiently trained workers, and awful parental awareness deprived almost 10–20% infants, who received initial dose of TOV (Trivalent Oral Vaccine), of getting their second and third booster doses.[2]

[...]

Awful Parental Perception

Besides such unavoidable circumstances, refusal of parents to get their children immunize (up to 74%) is another key issue as observed in Karachi in the last two latest SIAs. Pashtuns from low as well as high income group refuse to get their children vaccinated. Due to scarcity of polio awareness, trust deficiency in vaccine efficacy, vaccine related misconceptions, and lack of confidence on polio workers, Pashtuns of low income group have been found to be more reluctant in getting immunized in SIAs, of their children in comparison to non-Pashtuns of low income group. Strong influence of a religious person is one of the other factors that makes the Pashtuns avoid or refuse vaccinating their children. Key to eradication lies in counseling the male members for being the driving force in decision making.[39, 40] Thus poor knowledge about vaccination is found to be the primary cause and religious misperceptions present in some ethnic groups are likely to be the secondary cause of a large group of population that remain unimmunized.[41]

Polio Resurgence: A Nightmare

Statistical data analysis showed that Pakistan had 5 NIDs (National Immunization Days) rounds along with sub-NIDs that were two in number in 2001 with 119 confirmed polio cases. Sind province had the highest number of cases (25 cases) as compared to Baluchistan (20 cases), Punjab (18 cases), and Khyber Pakhtunkhwa (22 cases). In the next year (2002) a falloff trend in numeric value of polio cases (90 confirmed cases) was seen. Year 2003 again showed a rising trend (103 new cases of polio). For the next four years the number showed variation between 59 and 32. Real difficulty started in year 2008 when number of cases touched triple figure of 118 cases. Reason behind that surge appeared to be that there is no conductance of SIAs due to security reasons in areas near porous Pakistan and Afghanistan border and vast areas of FATA and KPK. Moreover immunization campaigns were intensely affected in Baluchistan and Sind provinces due to political and administrative issues. For year 2009 a total number of reported cases of wild polio viral strains were 89.[2] Numerical and geographical resurgence spread trend is predominant since 2007 and thereafter which is quite clear from the situation of Punjab province harboring more than 60% population. It was polio-free in 2007 and unfortunately had 8 reported cases in year 2008.[42] Vaccination coverage has shown an increasing overall trend from 1980 to the first decade of 21st century. Apparently the number of polio cases should decrease and it was true until 2007 after which a rapid rise was recorded despite expanding immunization coverage.[22] Geographical unstable law and order situation looted that success and FATA became red zone for polio teams. Moreover mass movement of local population from these polio affected areas leads to sharp increase in wild polio virus cases to the highest number, with 144 cases in 2010 and 198 in 2011.[15] Out of total (144) reported cases in 2010, again, 100 cases were from conflict-affected regions of western border of the country (FATA had 23 cases while the rest were from KPK).[2] Significant progress was shown by Pakistan in year 2012 as number value decreased to just 58 cases in comparison to 198 cases of previous year.[22] Wild polio virus type 1 (WPV1) confirmed reported cases in year 2013 were 93 in comparison to 58 cases of previous year.[6] In 2014 Pakistan plunged into the deep sea of difficulties as the figure rose to red alert level of 328 of polio cases. It was a setback for eradication efforts. Year 2015 ended up with 56 WPV cases. Only two polio cases have been reported until February 2016. Polio resurgence has become a nightmare for people being linked to achieving eradication goal.[43]

Recommendations and Possible Way Outs

Despite various setbacks, the target is still not impossible. In India successful polio eradication has made history and has become a source of inspiration for South Asian countries that elimination is possible, even under tough circumstances. Financial aid and assistance should be there for resource-poor countries by GPEI and manufacturers of vaccines .[17] Indian polio eradication success can be utilized by the rest of endemic countries like Pakistan to achieve their remaining goals. Year 2010 proved to be a remarkable year in Indian history, as use of bOPV (bivalent oral polio vaccine) immunization strategy proved itself as a giant leap on bumpy polio eradication road. Strong surveillance network by trained staff [20] and effective ground level delivery system made eradication a reality.[48] It is recommended to vaccinate each child through high standard coverage rather than depending on NIDs only, which will help Pakistan to eradicate polio.[14] (2)Polio immunization campaigns may not be very much publicized because safety of heath workers is critical to eradication success.(3)Decisive fight strategy against polio epidemic needs to be worked out once again because of cVDPV (Circulating Vaccine Derived Polio Virus), use of IPV instead of OPV (cost and administration techniques), and plan for cessation of OPV.[49] (4)Health workers are frontline attack against polio, so making sure that they are safe is quite important in conflict harboring areas of country.[6] (5)Strengthening of surveillance network globally will certainly help to eradicate polio.[6] (6)Counseling of parents either through religious entities or parents participating in SIAs can serve as role model.[39] Strategy involving religious leaders has already been exercised in Nigeria and northern Indian region.[50, 51] (7)Communication strategies like social mobilization and interpersonal communication should be focused to target unimmunized population.[40] (8)Strategy having adaptability and learning experience would serve better in conflict harboring areas of country.[52]

Conclusion

Although Pakistan is well committed to eliminating polio still it has to go a long way. Revolutionary steps which are already present in black and white need to be translated into an effective strategy at ground level rather than only mourning the current situation. Indian success strategy can be followed. Tribal belt in the northwestern border of country has to be given special stress and policies based on ground realities should be designed to make eradication a reality.

Notes

1. P. D. Minor, "The polio-eradication programme and issues of the end game," Journal of General Virology, vol. 93, no. 3, pp. 457–474, 2012. View at Publisher · View at Google Scholar · View at Scopus

2. M. Shah, M. K. Khan, S. Shakeel et al., "Resistance of polio to its eradication in Pakistan," Virology Journal, vol. 8, article 457, 2011. View at Publisher · View at Google Scholar · View at Scopus

6. E. K. Moturi, K. A. Porter, S. G. F. Wassilak et al., "Progress toward polio eradication—worldwide, 2013-2014," Morbidity and Mortality Weekly Report, vol. 63, no. 21, pp. 468–472, 2014. View at Google Scholar · View at Scopus

7. B. Aylward and T. Yamada, "The polio endgame," The New England Journal of Medicine, vol. 364, no. 24, pp. 2273–2275, 2011. View at Publisher · View at Google Scholar · View at Scopus

8. T. D. Mangal, R. B. Aylward, M. Mwanza et al., "Key issues in the persistence of poliomyelitis in Nigeria: a case-control study," The Lancet Global Health, vol. 2, no. 2, pp. e90–e97, 2014. View at Publisher · View at Google Scholar · View at Scopus

9. C. Lahariya, "Global eradication of polio: the case for 'finishing the job'," Bulletin of the World Health Organization, vol. 85, no. 6, pp. 487–492, 2007. View at Publisher · View at Google Scholar · View at Scopus

10. M. Yahya, "Polio vaccines—'no thank you!' barriers to polio eradication in Northern Nigeria," African Affairs, vol. 106, no. 423, pp. 185–204, 2007. View at Publisher · View at Google Scholar · View at Scopus

11. L. Roberts, "Infectious disease. Vaccine-related polio outbreak in Nigeria raises concerns," Science, vol. 317, no. 5846, article 1842, 2007. View at Google Scholar

12. Centers for Disease Control and Prevention (CDC), "Progress toward poliomyelitis eradication—India, January 2006–September 2007," MMWR Morbidity and Mortality Weekly Report, vol. 56, no. 45, pp. 1187–1191, 2007. View at Google Scholar

13. Centers for Disease Control and Prevention (CDC), "Progress toward poliomyelitis eradication—Pakistan and Afghanistan, 2007," Morbidity and Mortality Weekly Report, vol. 57, no. 12, pp. 315–319, 2008. View at Google Scholar

14. I. Ahmad and H. Khan, "Polio free Pakistan: a goal yet to be achieved," Gomal Journal of Medical Sciences, vol. 12, no. 4, pp. 187–188, 2014. View at Google Scholar

15. A. Islam, A. Sial, and K. Rizwan, "Why polio eradication program was not successfully implemented in Pakistan?" Public Policy and Administration Research, vol. 3, pp. 79–86, 2013. View at Google Scholar

16. R. Jooma, "Polio travel restrictions: a sledgehammer to crack a nut?" Pakistan Journal of Medical Sciences, vol. 30, no. 4, 2014. View at Publisher · View at Google Scholar · View at Scopus

17. Z. A. Bhutta and W. A. Orenstein, "Scientific declaration on polio eradication," Vaccine, vol. 31, no. 27, pp. 2850–2851, 2013.

20. N. Bhatnagar, M. Grover, S. Sinha, and R. Kaur, "Poliomyelitis eradication: rhetoric or reality," Asian Pacific Journal of Tropical Disease, vol. 3, no. 3, pp. 240–241, 2013.

22. T. Khan and J. Qazi, "Hurdles to the global antipolio campaign in Pakistan: an outline of the current status and future prospects to achieve a polio free world," Journal of Epidemiology and Community Health, vol. 67, no. 8, pp. 696–702, 2013.

23. L. Roberts, "Fighting polio in Pakistan," Science, vol. 337, no. 6094, pp. 517–521, 2012.

25. Pakistan: PolioOutbreak-2014–2016, http://reliefweb.int/report/pakistan/pakistan-violence-against-polio-campaigns-january-december-2015.

26. S. Closser and R. Jooma, "Why we must provide better support for Pakistan's female frontline health workers," PLoS Medicine, vol. 10, no. 10, Article ID e1001528, 2013. View at Publisher · View at Google Scholar · View at Scopus

27. S. Abimbola, A. U. Malik, and G. F. Mansoor, "The final push for polio eradication: addressing the challenge of violence in Afghanistan, Pakistan, and Nigeria," PLoS Medicine, vol. 10, article e1001529, 2013. View at Publisher · View at Google Scholar · View at Scopus

28. Z. A. Bhutta, "What must be done about the killings of Pakistani healthcare workers?" British Medical Journal, vol. 346, article f280, 2013. View at Publisher · View at Google Scholar · View at Scopus

29. J. Maurice, "Polio eradication effort sees progress, but problems remain," The Lancet, vol. 383, no. 9921, pp. 939–940, 2014. View at Publisher · View at Google Scholar · View at Scopus

30. D. McNeil, "CIA Vaccine Ruse in Pakistan May Have Harmed Polio Fight," The New York Times, 2012.

31. I. U. Din, Z. Mumtaz, and A. Ataullahjan, "How the Taliban undermined community healthcare in Swat, Pakistan," The British Medical Journal, vol. 344, Article ID e2093, 2012.

32. K. Ahmad, "Pakistan struggles to eradicate polio," The Lancet Infectious Diseases, vol. 7, no. 4, article 247, 2007. View at Publisher · View at Google Scholar · View at Scopus

33. M. U. Mushtaq, M. A. Majrooh, M. Z. S. Ullah et al., "Are we doing enough? Evaluation of the Polio Eradication Initiative in a district of Pakistan's Punjab province: a LQAS study," BMC Public Health, vol. 10, article 60, 2010. View at Publisher · View at Google Scholar · View at Scopus

34. S. Nishtar, "Pakistan, politics and polio," Bulletin of the World Health Organization, vol. 88, no. 2, pp. 159–160, 2010. View at Publisher · View at Google Scholar · View at Scopus

35. Q. Hasan, A. H. Bosan, and K. M. Bile, "A review of EPI progress in Pakistan towards achieving coverage targets: present situation and the way forward," Eastern Mediterranean Health Journal, vol. 16, pp. S31–S38, 2010.

39. A. R. Khowaja, S. A. Khan, N. Nizam, S. B. Omer, and A. Zaidi, "Parental perceptions surrounding polio and self-reported non-participation in polio supplementary immunization activities in Karachi, Pakistan: a mixed methods study," Bulletin of the World Health Organization, vol. 90, no. 11, pp. 822–830, 2012. View at Publisher · View at Google Scholar · View at Scopus

40. R. Obregón, K. Chitnis, C. Morry et al., "Achieving polio eradication: a review of health communication evidence and lessons learned in India and Pakistan," Bulletin of the World Health Organization, vol. 87, no. 8, pp. 624–630, 2009.

41. A. Sheikh, B. Iqbal, A. Ehtamam et al., "Reasons for non-vaccination in pediatric patients visiting tertiary care centers in a polio-prone country," Archives of Public Health, vol. 71, article 19, pp. 1–8, 2013. View at Publisher · View at Google Scholar

42. Y. B. Hadi and A. M. A. H. Sohail, "Pakistan: the nidus for global polio re-emergence?" Journal of Infection and Public Health, vol. 8, no. 2, pp. 214–215, 2015.

43. GPEI: Wild polio type 1 and circulating vaccine-derived polio cases, 2016, http://www.polioeradication.org/Dataandmonitoring/Poliothisweek.aspx.

48. O. Kew, "Reaching the last one per cent: progress and challenges in global polio eradication," Current Opinion in Virology, vol. 2, no. 2, pp. 188–198, 2012.

49. C. F. Estívariz, M. A. Pallansch, A. Anand et al., "Poliovirus vaccination options for achieving eradication and securing the endgame," Current Opinion in Virology, vol. 3, no. 3, pp. 309–315, 2013.

50. S. Chaturvedi, R. Dasgupta, V. Adhish et al., "Deconstructing social resistance to pulse polio campaign in two North Indian districts," Indian Pediatrics, vol. 46, no. 11, pp. 963–974, 2009. View at Google Scholar · View at Scopus

51. E. Renne, "Perspectives on polio and immunization in Northern Nigeria," Social Science & Medicine, vol. 63, no. 7, pp. 1857–1869, 2006.

52. D. Maher, "The human qualities needed to complete the global eradication of polio," Bulletin of the World Health Organization, vol. 91, no. 4, pp. 283–289, 2013.]

Evidence-Based Medicine Fights Back Against Misinformation

Julia Belluz

In the following excerpted viewpoint, Julia Belluz details the story of Hilda Bastian, now a health researcher whose previous beliefs—established in the 1980s—would currently be considered to fall under the umbrella of "fake news." Bastian was the head of an organization called Homebirth Australia, which argued against mothers giving birth in hospitals, suggesting instead they should do so in the comfort and safety of their own homes. Bastian had a change of heart when she discovered the facts that babies born at home in Australia faced higher mortality risk. The author details the importance of teaching people how to make informed health decisions while they are young, rather than when they are adults. Jullia Belluz is Vox's senior health correspondent, focused on medicine, science, and public health.

As you read, consider the following questions:

1. What is important about how Bastian switched from home birth advocate to critic?
2. What is more important, being credible or being trustworthy? Explain your reasoning.
3. Why is it important that doctors make information both reliable and easily accessed? And what does "easy access" mean?

L ong before Hilda Bastian was a health researcher, she endorsed a practice she believes may have cost lives.

"I think people died because of me," she said recently. "And I'll spend my whole life trying not to do it again and to make amends."

In the 1980s, Bastian was skeptical of the medical establishment. As the head of Homebirth Australia, she traveled the country and appeared on TV programs arguing that moms should have their babies outside the cold confines of hospital rooms.

Then she learned babies born at home in Australia faced a higher mortality risk than those born in hospital at that time. The fact disturbs her to this day.

In the decades since, she's become one of the most prominent thinkers in the world on scientific literacy and evidence-based medicine. She has dedicated her life to figuring out how to reach people with the best available health research and fight back against misinformation.

For her and many other health researchers and doctors, "fake news" and misinformation—problems that suddenly seem dire in light of Donald Trump's election and the growing influence of sites like Alex Jones's Infowars—are nothing new. And over the past 30 years, mostly under a movement called "evidence-based medicine," they've come with up with tools and techniques to fight back against bunk. They've also learned hard lessons on what doesn't work when it comes to using facts to change people's minds and behaviors.

Their lessons can help all of us—journalists, policymakers, teachers, educators, and even just concerned citizens talking to friends over the dinner table—who care about evidence and want to empower others with it.

Lesson 1: Take Time to Explain Why You Believe Something—Not Just What You Believe and Why Your Opponent Is Wrong

So how did Bastian switch over from home birth advocate to home birth critic?

It started with conversations with researchers in Sydney, who were compassionate about her worldview and generous with their time.

In the 1980s, Bastian went to a workshop at a childbirth education conference and met a researcher, Judith Lumley, who wanted to help her understand medical evidence. Through Lumley, Bastian connected with others in the scientific community who took the time to explain not only the evidence behind home birthing but also how to understand its strengths and limitations.

[…]

In that process, Bastian learned that you can't simply change minds by telling people that what they believe is wrong and you have the correct information. If those researchers had gone after her and shouted about their beliefs, Bastian probably would have deepened her stance in opposition.

Over time, Bastian said, the researchers convinced her "by being credible and trustworthy," not just appealing to emotion. They even inspired her to get into science. (By the late 1990s, the "proud high school dropout" was publishing research articles on mortality risks related to home births; she's now on staff at the National Institutes of Health and working on her PhD—her first degree.)

When you win people over this way, Bastian added, it can take a while—but you're more likely to bring others from the opposing community along. In her case, she stuck around Homebirth

Australia, helping to get the practice regulated and develop national guidelines on safe home birthing.

This process wasn't easy. Bastian received death threats for her change of heart, and the harassment went on for years. Not everyone in the home birthing community appreciated her push for higher standards.

Through her experience, she thinks there's a lesson for people trying to fight against people skeptical of scientific evidence, like the anti-vaccine crusaders.

"[Pro-vaccine advocates] act as though there's certainty about the effects of vaccines when there isn't," she said. "And each time they do that, they let their side down. If you're on the anti side, you can just drive a bus through the holes in their arguments, and people are doing that."

Of course, all medical treatments—including vaccines—carries risks and side effects, and sometimes vaccine advocates are too quick to pretend that research doesn't exist. "It's fighting bias with bias and it doesn't work," Bastian says. "It just creates more bias and polarizes people." Instead, taking time to explain why you believe something—not just what you believe and why your opponent is wrong—can go a long way.

Lesson 2: Make Sure Your Information Is Reliable and Easy to Access

In order to talk to others about evidence, you need to sort out which evidence is reliable, and find ways to make it readily accessible and understandable. And the evidence-based medicine movement, which started to catch on in the early 1990s, developed tools to do just that.

Back then, doctors were too often using single or cherry-picked studies, or what they learned in medical school or from their mentors, to inform their decisions about their patients' best care. These one-off studies and old lesson plans didn't always represent of the totality of the research.

So a group of doctors, researchers, and patients began to organize themselves to solve the problem: to figure out how to sort evidence, and get all the best research digested for doctors so they could use it at the bedside when they needed it, rather than just relying on whatever study they came across that day or what their mentors told them.

These researchers built up a repository of high-quality "systematic reviews," most notably through the Cochrane Collaboration. The reviews used statistical methods to bring together and sort all the best science on specific medical questions, and presented that evidence in a coherent summary.

This effort was revolutionary. Systematic reviews added empirical heft to medicine. They helped doctors more easily access and make sense of a wider selection of data, and they often corrected misconceptions about important health issues—like the advice that it was best to put newborns to sleep on their stomachs, a practice that actually increased babies' risk of death.

But Bastian—one of the founding Cochrane members—said she realized pretty quickly that the group had to reach beyond doctors and find ways to connect with other communities if they really wanted to have an impact. By 1999, she'd helped get "plain language summaries" added to Cochrane reviews. These summaries appear outside the paywall and articulate, in a few jargon-free sentences, the findings of a systematic review.

[…]

Lesson 3: Teach Them While They're Young

Just making high-quality evidence more available doesn't always stop bogus claims from taking off, of course, and many people often lack the tools to think critically about the information they're given.

That's a problem Andy Oxman, a researcher based in Norway who has studied how to help people make informed health choices for more than 30 years, has become obsessed with. After working with health professionals, journalists, and policymakers over the decades, he noticed that "most adults don't have time to learn, and they have to unlearn a lot of stuff."

So he started to wonder whether children might be more amenable subjects for learning how to assess evidence and claims. To put this idea to the test, in 2000 he visited his then-10-year-old son's class.

"I told them that some teenagers had discovered that red M&Ms gave them a good feeling in their body and helped them write and draw more quickly," Oxman said. "But there also were some bad effects: a little pain in their stomach, and they got dizzy if they stood up quickly."

He challenged the kids to try to find out if the teens were right. He split the class into small groups and gave each group a bag of M&Ms.

The kids quickly figured out they had to try eating M&Ms of different colors to find out what happens, but that it wouldn't be a fair test if they could see the color of the M&Ms. In other words, they intuitively understood the concept of "blinding" in a clinical trial. (This is when researchers prevent study participants and doctors from knowing who got what treatment so they're less likely to be biased about the outcome.)

Within an hour of grappling over how to test the M&Ms, the children seemed to grasp basic concepts about testing health claims. "That convinced me that's the age to start," Oxman said.

So he's been working with other researchers from around the world to develop curricula—cartoon-filled books, podcasts— for schoolchildren on how to instill critical thinking skills at an early age. He's tested their impact in a big trial involving 15,000 schoolchildren in Uganda.

We don't yet know whether this method will work because the results haven't been published—but whether or not the trial fails, it'll bring us closer to answering an important question about information right now: How do you prevent dubious claims from catching on in the first place?

Stanford University professor John Ioannidis also sees the most hope in early childhood education, and agrees children should be empowered with basic skills on critical thinking. He told me that waiting to teach clinicians the standards of evidence-based medicine late in their training doesn't always work.

"They've already been exposed to things that are so un-evidence-based, and the same principle applies to the general public," he says. "We need to start early on, to make people understand that basing decisions on fair tests, on science, on evidence is important." He would like to see basic courses on how to seek out high-quality information and appraise it taught alongside math and reading.

Lesson 4: Evidence Is Necessary but Not Sufficient

Leonard Syme, considered the father of social epidemiology, helped invent a critical field of health research. But he also looks back and thinks many of his efforts over the years failed because researchers like him were too out of touch with the needs of the people they were trying to influence.

In the early 1970s, he started running a 10-year, $555 million study that involved 350,000 people. The focus: changing participants' behaviors on three risk factors—high cholesterol, high blood pressure, and smoking—that the scientific community knew increased the risk of disease and death.

"I devoted 10 years of my life to that project," Syme said. "When the results came up with no change at all—nobody changed behavior!—that was really shattering for me."

Another study, based in a community in Richmond, California, also focused on different interventions to get people to cut back on smoking. After five years, again, they had made no dent in the smoking rate.

Syme did some soul searching. He reflected on how Richmond's economy centered on ship yards that sent food and ammunitions to the Europe during World War II. When the war ended, the city had been left without jobs, in poverty. "There's air pollution, high crime," he said. "The city's devastated."

"If you ask the people there what problems were on their mind, I promise you smoking would not be on their list. But I didn't pay attention to that because I was a public health expert."

It occurred to him that public health experts needed to meet people where they are and better connect to their contexts.

"The cold, hard statistics I trained in just don't do it," Syme said. Or, as Benjamin Djulbegovic, a cancer researcher and evidence-based medicine thinker at the University of South Florida, put it: "Evidence is necessary but not sufficient for decision making or changing behaviors."

[…]

Periodical and Internet Sources Bibliography

The following articles have been selected to supplement the diverse views presented in this chapter.

Advisory Board, "'Fake medical news' has a 'body count,' one doctor warns. Here's how to fight back." Advisory Board, December 21, 2018. https://www.advisory.com/daily-briefing/2018/12/21/fake-news.

Jeremy D. Bailoo, "Celebrating #WorldImmunizationWeek – The MMR-Andrew Wakefield Scandal," Speaking of Research, April 23, 2019. https://speakingofresearch.com/2019/04/23/celebrating-world-vaccination-week-pt-2-the-mmr-andrew-wakefield-scandal/.

Julia Bruckner, "Fake News Happens in Medicine Too," Op-Med, March 13, 2019. https://opmed.doximity.com/articles/fake-news-happens-in-medicine-too.

Tabi Jackson Gee, "Is Dr Instagram ruining your health?" *Telegraph*, April 7, 2019. https://www.telegraph.co.uk/health-fitness/body/dr-instagram-ruining-health/.

Kayla Glaraton, "Celebrities Helped Create the Measles Epidemic, Who Will Stop Them?" Pavlovic Today, May 14, 2019. https://www.thepavlovictoday.com/celebrities-helped-create-the-measles-epidemic-who-will-stop-them/.

Soumya Karlamangla, "Measles' next target in Los Angeles: Unvaccinated college students," *LA Times*, April 23, 2019. https://www.latimes.com/local/lanow/la-me-ln-measles-outbreaks-los-angeles-colleges-20190423-story.html.

Haq Nawaz Khan and Pamela Constable, "Pakistan had all but eliminated polio. Then things went badly wrong." *Washington Post*, May 10, 2019. https://www.washingtonpost.com/world/asia_pacific/pakistan-had-all-but-eliminated-polio-then-things-went-badly-wrong/2019/05/10/87f328e8-711c-

11e9-9331-30bc5836f48e_story.html?noredirect=on&utm_
term=.212f30696139.

Soumya Karlamangla, "Measles' next target in Los Angeles:
Unvaccinated college students," *LA Times*, April 23, 2019. https://
www.latimes.com/local/lanow/la-me-ln-measles-outbreaks-los-
angeles-colleges-20190423-story.html.

Lucy Lamble, "The women defying menace and mistrust to rid
Pakistan of polio," *Guardian*, May 14, 2019. https://www.
theguardian.com/global-development/2019/may/14/the-women-
defying-menace-and-mistrust-to-rid-pakistan-of-polio.

Caitlin Oprysko, "Trump: People 'have to get their shots' amid
measles crisis," Politico, April 26, 2019. https://www.politico.com/
story/2019/04/26/trump-vaccines-measles-crisis-1290720.

Logan Raschke, "Historical, modern perspectives of
vaccination controversy," Daily Eastern News, May 12, 2019.
https://www.dailyeasternnews.com/2019/05/12/historical-
modern-perspectives-of-vaccination-controversy/.

T. S. Sathyanarayana Rao and Chittaranjan Andrade, "The MMR
vaccine and autism: Sensation, refutation, retraction, and fraud,"
Indian J Psychiatry, April-June 2011. https://www.ncbi.nlm.nih.
gov/pmc/articles/PMC3136032/.

Staff Reports, "ANOTHER VIEWPOINT: Measles is back and we
only have ourselves to blame," Greenfield Reporter, May 10,
2019. http://www.greenfieldreporter.com/2019/05/11/another_
viewpoint_measles_is_back_and_we_only_have_ourselves_to_
blame/.

Sabrina Toppa, "Anti-vaxxers stand in way of Pakistan's final fight
against polio," *Al Jazeera*, May 14, 2019. https://www.aljazeera.
com/indepth/features/anti-vaxxers-stand-pakistan-final-fight-
polio-190513121511307.html.

GLOBALVIEWPOINTS

CHAPTER

What Are the Causes of the Rise of Mental Health Disorders Around the World?

Around the World a Mental Health Stigma Persists

Prashant Bharadwaj, Mallesh Pai, Agne Suziedelyte

In the following viewpoint, Prashant Bharadwaj, Mallesh Pai, and Agne Suziedelyte detail how certain stigmas lead individuals to hide certain behaviors or actions, primarily in regard to the treatment of mental health ailments. In 2012, 18.6 percent of adults in the United States reported having a recent mental illness, a metric that is similar in other countries around the world. But with the high levels of under-reporting or misreporting, the number of people who actually have a diagnosable mental disorder is much more difficult to quantify. It is a no-win situation, where people who do not seek treatment for their illnesses suffer just as much as the people who do. Prashant Bharadwaj is associate professor economics at UC San Diego. Mallesh Pai is assistant professor in economics at the University of Pennsylvania. Agne Suziedelyte is research fellow at the Centre for Health Economics at Monash University.

As you read, consider the following questions:

1. According to the viewpoint, why would mental illness be ranked at the bottom in terms of public perception?
2. What is the most significant financial impact of the stigma around mental health?
3. Why is it more likely a person would mis-report or under-report having a mental disorder?

The fear of being stigmatised or socially sanctioned and disgraced governs many aspects of human behaviour. In many cases, the fear of stigma does not result in actual behavioural change but rather leads individuals to hide certain behaviours or actions (for example, smoking in secrecy). Despite the centrality and importance of stigma in influencing human behaviour, formal treatments of it in economics have been limited. However, it is commonly agreed that stigma exists and influences behaviour in many spheres.

In 2012, 18.6% of all US adults had a recent mental illness.1 The prevalence is similar in other developed countries. Studies show that public knowledge about mental health illnesses has recently increased, but considerable stigmatisation of individuals with mental health illnesses remains. For example, mental illness is ranked near the bottom of other illnesses in terms of public acceptance (Hinshaw 2007). As a result, the negative effects of stigma have been hypothesised to be as harmful as the direct effect of mental disorder (Hinshaw 2007). According to the US Surgeon General report, stigma is the main barrier to mental health care: "It deters the public from seeking, and wanting to pay for, care" (US Department of Health and Human Services 1999). Hence, stigma could prevent individuals from seeking care, leading to more intense (and perhaps less successful) and expensive treatment options later (Kupfer et al. 1989). In our research, we set out to show the existence and consequences of stigma in the case of mental health (Bharadwaj 2015).

Modelling Stigmatisation

In line with a classic definition of stigma (Goffman 1963), we build a simple model in which agents with traits that are stigmatised by society want to hide these traits from others. In particular, agents face costs if traits that are stigmatised if revealed publicly, but they also face costs for not reporting truthfully. However, in each situation where the agent is asked about whether she has a certain stigmatised condition (an example is a survey), she is unable to determine whether her answer will be made public (i.e., privacy concerns). Hence, coarse perception regarding the cost of truthful reporting can generate relatively greater misreporting for traits that are stigmatised, even on surveys where anonymity is assured.

We show evidence of this 'hiding' behaviour for mental health problems by comparing survey self-reports on diagnoses and mental health drug use to administrative data on prescription drug use from Australia. While there could be various drivers for the differences between survey self-reports and administrative data, our leading explanation is that if mental illnesses were not stigmatised, the difference between self-reported survey responses and objective administrative records should be statistically similar to other diseases. Our operational definition of stigma is quite broad, and aggregates causes such as shame, guilt, self-image, and concerns for social discrimination, but we are able to specifically separate out labour market discrimination concerns.

- We find that approximately 36% of individuals whom we observe with a diagnosis of depression self-report as not having a mental disorder.

The degree of misreporting is lower when individuals self-report prescription drug use for depression (20%).

- In contrast, people under-report other diagnoses, such as cardiovascular diseases and diabetes, about 18% and 11% of the time, respectively (14% and 13%, respectively, in the case of self-reported prescription drug use).

The Global Gag Rule

The same year the *Roe v. Wade* decision struck down anti-abortion laws in the United States, American policy toward abortions beyond our borders took major steps in the opposite direction. In 1973, Sen. Jesse Helms (R-NC) lobbied hard to secure the passage of a law that remains in force today: The Helms Amendment to the Foreign Assistance Act forbids the U.S. government from funding abortion procedures abroad.

In 1984, at an international conference on family planning in Mexico City, President Ronald Reagan imposed further restrictions on U.S. funds and international abortion-related activities through a regulation known as the Mexico City Policy or the Global Gag Rule. As originally written, it prevents any family planning foreign aid funds from going to hospitals and NGOs that perform or "actively promote" abortions—even if the organizations use non-U.S. funding to carry out such activities as informing patients of medically indicated options or working to reduce unsafe procedures.

Because it's an executive order, the White House doesn't have to go to Congress to change its stance on the Global Gag Rule. As a result, "it's a policy that ping-pongs every time the party in power at the White House changes," says Wendy Chavkin, professor emerita of Population and Family Health and Obstetrics-Gynecology and co-founder of Global Doctors for Choice. In place under Reagan and both President Bushes, the Mexico City Policy was rescinded by Presidents Clinton and Obama; on January 23, one of new President Trump's first actions in office was to sign an executive order putting it back in place.

Impact of the Global Gag Rule

The back-and-forth nature of the policy's history allowed public health researchers to understand the Global Gag Rule's impact on women's health around the world. The World Health Organization analyzed abortion rates across 20 countries, comparing datasets from the Clinton Administration with the following eight years under Bush, when the policy was reinstated. Their findings, published in 2011, are stark: in countries where the Mexico City Policy had the most impact, the number of abortions—both safe and unsafe—rose, while contraception use fell.

"The Global Gag Rule Returns, And Could Be More Harmful
Than Ever," Columbia University, January 31, 2017.

These Differences Are Statistically Significant

Our sample is unique in that about 25% of the population are migrants to Australia. When examining the degree of under-reporting by country of origin, our results suggest that individuals from Asia and the Middle East are more likely to under-report relative to individuals from Northern Europe or the Americas. There is also a steep age gradient in misreporting, with older people more likely to misreport than younger people. Males are more likely to misreport compared to females.

We provide suggestive evidence that stigma is likely to play a role in the decision to seek treatment by examining the characteristics of people who self-report as having mental health issues according to a commonly used measure (the Kessler Psychological Distress scale), but do not seek mental health treatment in the subsequent 12 months. The overlap of socioeconomic and demographic characteristics that predict both under-reporting conditional on seeking care and not seeking care conditional on a high probability of having mental health problems, is suggestive of the role that stigma plays in preventing health care seeking.

Non-Stigma Related Hiding Behaviours

It is important to recognise that not all forms of hiding behaviour or trait concealment are the result of stigma. For example, individuals might lie on a survey given by an employer by showing extra years of experience or misreporting other information, including mental health history, to get a higher wage or a promotion. This sort of strategic reporting could be motivated by an individual's concern of stigma as well as labour market discrimination. Our results are interpretable as evidence of stigma in mental health if we assume that the labour market discrimination motive in misreporting is similar across various diseases, such as diabetes or hypertension. Hence, the relative excess misreporting in mental health is evidence of stigma. Importantly, our sample consists of a large number of non-employed individuals, mainly retirees, for whom we can plausibly claim that the labour market discrimination motive is weak. For this subsample, our reliance on the homogeneity of the labour market discrimination motive is mitigated.

There could also be a general concern about survey reporting error that is driven by inattention, recall, lack of clear communication between doctors and patients, etc. (see Bound et al. 2001 for a comprehensive list). Such general explanations for differences in survey and administrative data records lead us to test a few hypotheses.

- First, these general explanations might result in all diseases and conditions being under-reported to a similar extent. This is contradicted by the data.

- Second, differential misreporting remains when we change the recall window over which we compare survey reports to administrative data, suggesting that simple recall issues are not driving our results.

- Third, our results are robust to analysis that is akin to a fixed-effect model; an individual who is treated for both cardiovascular disease and depression, for example, is much more likely to under-report his mental health condition relative to his heart condition.

- Fourth, doctor fixed effects regressions leave the results largely unchanged; hence, doctor-specific communication strategies are not driving our results.

- Finally, while some anti-depressants might be used for conditions other than depression, institutional insurance reasons and other robustness tests suggest that this is extremely unlikely to be driving our results.

Our work complements a recent set of papers in economics that focus on stigma in the case of HIV (Thornton 2008, Derksen et al. 2014, Hoffmann et al. 2014, Ngatia 2011).2 Using randomised control trials, these papers highlight the role of incentives, information, and social networks in understanding and mitigating the negative consequences of HIV-related stigma.

Our paper is also related to other papers that match self-reported health measures to administrative health records (Barker et al. 2004, Johnston et al. 2009). In a review of papers comparing self-reports to medical data, Harlow and Linet (1989) find that most papers focus on reproductive health; no examples of such comparisons in the mental health space are cited. Finally, our paper is also related to the literature examining the degree of misreporting in other government programmes and in surveys.3 In a general review of measurement error in surveys, Bound et al. (2001) discuss the possibility of 'social desirability' influencing how data could be misreported. Thus, our paper adds evidence to this literature on measurement error in surveys by providing evidence on misreporting along an important variable of public health concern. By contrasting with other diseases, we also posit a possible mechanism (stigma) for systematic excess under-reporting for socially undesirable traits. In that sense, our analysis is related to the literature seeking to document and understand social desirability bias using other methods in different settings (Coffman et al. 2013).

Concluding Remarks

The most important facet of stigma that pertains to public health policy is the extent to which it might prevent individuals from seeking appropriate care. Our results show that stigma concerns can play a significant role in determining health care seeking behaviour in the case of mental health. To the extent that policy or broader market forces can reduce stigma in mental health, our conclusions suggest that this will lead to more individuals seeking and obtaining treatment, and eventually lessening the burden of the disease.

References

Almada, L, I M McCarthy, and R Tchernis (2015), "What Can We Learn About the Effects of Food Stamps on Obesity in the Presence of Misreporting?", SSRN.

Baker, M, M Stabile, and C Deri (2004), "What do self-reported, objective, measures of health measure?", Journal of Human Resources, 39(4), 1067-1093.

Bharadwaj, P, M P Pai and A Suziedelyte (2015), "Mental Health Stigma", NBER Working Paper 21240.

Bound, J, C Brown, and N Mathiowetz (2001), "Measurement error in survey data", Handbook of Econometrics, 5, 3705-3843.

Coffman, K B, L C Coffman, and K M M Ericson (2013), "The size of the LGBT population and the magnitude of anti-gay sentiment are substantially underestimated", NBER Working Paper 19508.

Derksen, L, A Muula, and J van Oosterhout (2014), "Love in the Time of HIV: Theory and Evidence on Social Stigma and Health Seeking Behaviour", Working Paper, London School of Economics.

Goffman, E (1963), Stigma: Notes on the management of spoiled identity, Simon and Schuster.

Harlow, S D, and M S Linet (1989), "Agreement between questionnaire data and medical records: the evidence for accuracy of recall", American Journal of Epidemiology, 129(2), 233-48.

Hinshaw, S P (2007), The mark of shame: Stigma of mental illness and agenda for change, Oxford University Press, New York.

Hoffmann, V, J R Fooks, and K D Messer (2014), "Measuring and Mitigating HIV Stigma: A Framed Field Experiment", Economic Development and Cultural Change, 62(4), 701-726.

Johnston, D W, C Propper, and M A Shields (2009), "Comparing subjective and objective measures of health: Evidence from hypertension for the income/health gradient", Journal of Health Economics, 28(3), 540-552.

Kupfer, D J, E Frank, and J M Perel (1989), "The advantage of early treatment intervention in recurrent depression", Archives of General Psychiatry, 46(9), 771–775.

Mahajan, A P, J N Sayles, V A Patel, R H Remien, D Ortiz, G Szekeres, and T J Coates (2008), "Stigma in the HIV/AIDS epidemic: a review of the literature and recommendations for the way forward", AIDS (London, England), 22(Suppl 2), S67.

Marquis, K H, and J C Moore (2010), "Measurement errors in SIPP program reports", Research Report Series, Survey Methodology

#2010-01, Statistical Research Division U.S. Census Bureau Washington, D.C.

Meyer, B D, W K Mok, and J X Sullivan (2009), "The under-reporting of transfers in household surveys: its nature and consequences", NBER Working Paper 15181.

Ngatia, M (2011), "Social interactions and individual reproductive decisions," Working Paper, Yale University.

Thornton, R L (2008), "The demand for, and impact of, learning HIV status," The American Economic Review, 98(5), 1829.

U S Department of Health and Human Services (1999), "Mental Health: A Report of the Surgeon General", Rockville, MD: U.S. Department of Health and Human Services, Substance Abuse and Mental Health Services Administration, Center for Mental Health Services, National Institutes of Health, National Institute of Mental Health.

Footnotes

1 http://www.nimh.nih.gov/health/statistics/prevalence/ any-mental-illness-ami-among-adults.shtml

2 There is certainly a broader, multidisciplinary set of papers on the issue of stigma in HIV. See Mahajan et al. (2008) for an excellent review.

3 Almada et al. (2015) provide some excellent examples of such work in the case of the Supplemental Nutrition Assistance Programme (SNAP). For example, Marquis and Moore (2010) show the extent of under-reporting of SNAP receipt in the Survey of Income and Programme Participation (SIPP) by comparing self-reports to administrative records. See also Meyer et al. (2009) for measures of under-reports in other transfer programs in the US.]

In Nepal There Is a Treatment Gap for Mental Health Problems

Mark JD Jordans, Nagendra P. Luitel, Mark Tomlinson, and Ivan H. Komproe

In the following excerpted viewpoint, Mark JD Jordans, Nagendra P. Luitel, Mark Tomlinson, and Ivan H. Komproe examine the lack of mental health treatment in Nepal. The authors note that there are several barriers to treatment, such as limited funds, lack of sufficient mental health specialists, and stigma. These challenges tend to exist in other low- and middle-income countries, as well. The authors explore potential pathways to overcome these barriers. Mark JD Jordans is affiliated with HealthNet TPO in Amsterdam and the Center for Global Mental Health at King's College London. Nagendra P. Luitel is in the research department of the Transcultural Psychosocial Organization in Nepal. Mark Tomlinson is in the Psychology Department of Stellenbosch University in South Africa. Ivan H. Komproe is affiliated with HealthNet TPO in Amersterdam and Utrecht University in the Netherlands.

"Setting Priorities for Mental Health Care in Nepal: A Formative Study," by Mark JD Jordans, Nagendra P. Luitel, Mark Tomlinson, and Ivan H. Komproe, BMC Psychiatry, December 5, 2013, https://bmcpsychiatry.biomedcentral.com/articles/10.1186/1471-244X-13-332. Licensed under CC BY 2.0.

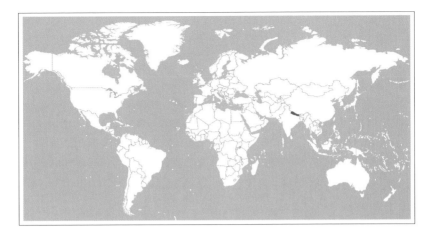

As you read, consider the following questions:

1. What is TOC according to the viewpoint?
2. Why is it important that families be included in the treatment paths?
3. In what other post-conflict countries has decentralized mental health care been advocated, according to the viewpoint?

Mental health needs of people in low and middle income countries are largely unmet, with only a small fraction of those affected receiving adequate treatment [1, 2]. The ambition of providing mental health care is beset by multiple challenges, which include limited mental health specialists and available treatments, often due to a lack of policies and financial resources [3]. There is an urgent need to identify effective strategies that overcome such barriers in the delivering interventions. The lack of this evidence is a major challenge in the process of scaling up mental health care in Low- and Middle Income Countries [4].

Multiple studies have demonstrated that interventions provided by trained non-specialists (i.e. task shifting) in low income settings can be effective in achieving significant treatment gain [5, 6, 7]. However, many of these are proof-of-concept studies as they remain relatively small-scale and treatment-specific. There is also a need for the implementation of packages of care that combine evidence-based treatments for multiple mental disorders rather than stand-alone interventions for single disorders [8]. To make significant progress in reducing the treatment gap, a comprehensive and multi-tiered approach is needed to bring evidence-based treatments to a national-level scale. With that aim, the World Health Organization has launched its mental health Gap Action Program (mhGAP) [9] which promotes the integration of mental health into primary health care.

The goal of developing population-wide mental health services in LMIC is not new. Previous programs have shown that practice-oriented mental health trainings for general health workers led to substantially increased uptake of mental health care services in Afghanistan [10]; while task-shifting has been shown to substantially reduce the human resource needs to address the treatment gap at minimal costs in South Africa [11]; and a large-scale mental health awareness program markedly increased referral to services in Nigeria [12]. At the same time, studies have demonstrated that training alone did little to improve the management of mental health problems [13]. Also in Nepal, there has been significant efforts made towards the development of a community mental health delivery program integrated in the public health system, yet without it being brought to scale [14]. The major challenge now is to know how best to address specific health systems constraints (including human resources, capacity building, information systems, health financing and service delivery), when trying to horizontally integrate mental health into primary care [15], given that there is no single best practice model available [16]. Consequently, there is an urgent need to better understand how a comprehensive mental health approach, encompassing services within primary health care and the surrounding community, can be developed and implemented.

The PRogramme for Improvement of Mental health carE (PRIME), a research consortium working in India, Uganda,

Ethiopia, South Africa and Nepal, aims to evaluate the feasibility, acceptability and impact of a multi-faceted mental health care approach that targets the health facility, community and health service organization [17]. Each site, in close partnership with Ministries of Health, will develop, implement, evaluate and scale-up a comprehensive mental health care plan.

While the development of a scalable model of mental health care is challenging in any LMIC, in fragile states or complex humanitarian emergencies this is particularly the case due to the increased risk of mental health problems [18, 19], and poor pre-existing health systems [20]. The present study is part of the formative phase of PRIME, which concentrates on assessing the priorities, processes and building blocks of developing such mental health care plan. The aim of the current study is to investigate the challenges and opportunities for the development and fine-tuning of a comprehensive mental health care plan in post-conflict Nepal. The study follows a combined methods design that includes a priority setting study, running workshops to develop a Theory of Change (TOC) and conducting a qualitative study.

[…]

Results

The disorders with highest ranking scores were depressive disorder, alcohol use disorder, epilepsy, anxiety disorder and psychoses—all of which had a total priority score of .75 and higher. The other disorders all had a markedly lower score on perceived treatment feasibility. In addition, the four disorders with the lowest collective agreement—developmental disorders, PTSD, behavioral disorders and dementia—also had low scores (.50 and lower) on cultural relevance.

After four consecutive workshops conducted alternatively with (mental) health care providers and policy makers, a final Theory of Change map was drawn up. In the TOC methodology, only the final outcome was decided a priori as 'improved social economic and health of people with mental disorders treated by the program.'

The first workshop developed a broad outline of preconditions related to service delivery, problem identification and detection, mental health literacy and stigma reduction, capacity building, quality assurance mechanisms, budget availability and political buy-in. The TOC formulated at this stage included a pathway for outcomes and associated interventions within the health facilities that focus mainly on the capacity of health care workers to identify, treat and follow-up with patients. This pathway was combined with questions about the additional burden the proposed activities would pose on health staff. Another pathway was aimed at the community, which involved training community volunteers in identification, sensitization and providing support to people with mental health problems. Related to this, respondents emphasized the need to systematically include families, peer and schools in the process. The availability of community-level service delivery agents was seen as the most important hurdle. A third pathway within the overall TOC concerned outcomes related to the functioning of the health organization. These included the establishment of a supervision system and the policy for procurement of psychotropic medications. Respondents were particularly concerned about the feasibility of a regular and reliable drug supply chain. Fine-tuning of the TOC in subsequent workshops resulted in recommendations towards the inclusion of preliminary outcomes or interventions related to livelihoods, rehabilitation, referral mechanisms and technical oversight, as well as defining assumptions around the participation of service users and adopting an approach combining pharmacological treatment with community-based psychosocial support mechanisms.

[...]

A number of overlapping and crosscutting themes emerged from the qualitative data. These included the negative attitudes that surround mental health that are pervasive, that permeate all sections of society, and which are particularly difficult to tackle. Negative attitudes result in discrimination of people with mental health problems, and underlie problems related to detection, low demand and access to services and perceived feasibility of task-shifting. While increasing mental health literacy was a much-advocated strategy to overcome these attitudes, respondents were unequivocal that much depends on what information is imparted to whom. For instance, information about availability of services should be disseminated publicly, yet a better understanding of mental health problems should be addressed in more private spheres. Also, working with people that are generally trusted (e.g. community elders and traditional healers) in combination with people who are respected public figures (e.g. celebrities and political activists) would expectedly sort the largest impact. The situation presented was even more nuanced, as education and awareness alone were found to be insufficient to actually change attitudes, as that required actual involvement of key stakeholders with mental health issues.

A recurrent theme was that for a mental health care plan to be introduced there is an urgent need to improve access to services. Having treatment available in itself would not guarantee access and uptake of such services. Community members stated that it was a necessity that health workers were sensitive and maintained confidential when dealing with people with mental health problems. They also pointed towards a need to change the commonly held notion that services at the health posts are for the poor and that the more affluent should go to the district hospital. But also more practical concerns would need to be addressed in order to improve access. For instance, health workers reported that the detection of people with mental health problems is fraught with difficulties, in part due to the low mental health literacy and persistent negative attitudes, also and especially in the people closest to people with mental health problems. Still, many respondents believed that lay people, especially after receiving training, would be able to identify that something was wrong, even if not able to identify the type of mental health problems. However, in the absence of specialized resources in the community, respondents stressed that health workers are ultimately responsible for the detecting mental illness. Access can further be increased by more pragmatic measures that were proposed during several of the interviews by community members and health workers, such as arranging support for the recurrent transport to and from the health facilities. Efforts to improve identification and access need to be sensitive to unhelpful sentiments among both help seekers and health providers. Currently, the former feared accusations and discrimination and therefor hid their problems, while the latter feared anger and aggressivity from patients.

In many of the processes involved in the establishment of a mental health care plan the families of people with mental health problems play a crucial, albeit dual, role. Families appeared to be somewhat of a double edged sword. On the one end, families were seen as the key agents to help in improving the detection, access and maintenance of mental health treatment and care. On the other hand, family members, due to fear for loss of status or being discriminated against, take part in the ill-treatment or neglect that patients experience. For example the family members were reported to restrict access to care by protecting the client from stigmatization and hostility by hiding the illness; others were reported to threaten to reject him or her from the family all together.

Numerous issues were raised by the respondents with regards to making task-shifting feasible and acceptable. Beyond the obvious need for training, all respondents emphasized the risk of over-burdening health workers and the need for compensations for all those involved in task-shifting. The formal recognition of training and mandate of the work was for many health workers as important as financial reimbursement. According to the majority of respondents people in the community should also be trained in mental health care, rather than health workers alone. It was suggested to have focal points in each village, or for every 15–20 households, who can play a role in the care and support of people with mental health problems.

Discussion

The literature on the integration of mental health into primary health care in LMIC is characterized by description of lessons learned from actual practice. To date, there is little formative research done in this area. The present study describes a systematic approach integrating formative research that provides data to inform the development of a comprehensive mental health care plan, incorporating the different perspectives of key stakeholders. We believe that a comprehensive methodology to identify and address barriers to acceptability and feasibility is important especially when applying mental health interventions cross-culturally [27]. The present combined-methods used in the formative research allows for the exploration of contextual knowledge of needed processes to put such plan into practice. In Nepal, a fragile state grappling with the aftermath of a decade of war and where even the most basic mental health services are unavailable in rural settings, this endeavor is met with many systemic obstacles. Health workers that are already overburdened, the unavailability of psychotropic medicines, and general unawareness of, or deeply engrained negative attitudes towards, people with mental health problems are some of the challenges introduced by stakeholders. At the same time however, developing mental health services anew also provides with opportunities to systematically build new structures [16]. The ability to plan for mental health services to take place concomitantly within the health facilities as well as the communities is a good example of this. The present study reveals the value of such a hybrid community-facility approach that includes a spectrum of interventions from tailor-made community sensitization and mobilizing community support to training health workers and a reliable supply of psychotropic drugs.

A strategy for decentralized mental health care has also been advocated in other post conflict settings such as Burundi [28],Uganda [29] and Lebanon [30]. While some initiatives towards a community mental health model have been implemented, or are presently ongoing, in Nepal [14, 31], the government has not yet, policy notwithstanding, adopted a plan for the integration of mental health into primary health care.

As the systematic introduction of community mental health care cannot, from the onset, feasibly target all disorders, prioritization is required. Should governments choose to target the disorders that are most prevalent, those that cause most burden or those that can be addressed most feasibly? As such decision has potentially large implications for the country's mental health strategy, it is important to have such prioritization done by key stakeholders in Nepal. The PRIME consortium has opted for depression disorder, alcohol use disorder and psychoses as priority disorders exactly because these impose the largest burden of disease and culturally acceptable interventions supported with robust evidence for effectiveness exists [17]. The results of the prioritization exercise, based on criteria of feasibility, acceptability and commonness, are largely congruent with those, except for the high priority given to epilepsy. The high importance given to epilepsy means that this will also be incorporated in the mental health care plan that is developed subsequent to this formative study.

The present study has a number of implications for the development of the mental health care plan in Nepal. The preliminary (i.e. before pilot-testing) care plan consists of different components. Within the community these included stigma reduction, sensitization, case detection, user group mobilization and focused psychosocial support. Within the health facility these included awareness raising, screening and assessment, pharmacological and psychosocial treatment, all of which are largely based on the mhGAP guidelines [9]. Training, drug-supply chain management, monitoring & evaluation and supervision are an integral part of the plan.

[…]

Conclusion

Our research has laid out a comprehensive framework for setting priorities for mental health care in Nepal. It has outlined major challenges as well as recommending concrete strategies about how to overcome them. There was a strong endorsement of a hybrid system that encompasses community-, and facility-based care. Guaranteeing a sustainable supply of psychotropic medicine and making sure to not over-burden health workers or volunteers were identified as key challenges. The dual capacity of families, both the natural sphere of support for people with mental health problems and the ones maintaining or reinforcing negative attitudes towards sufferers, was also seen as needing attention. This study provides the foundation for further development and evaluation of integrated mental health care in Nepal.

Notes

1. McBain R, Norton DJ, Morris J, Yasamy MT, Betancourt TS: The role of health systems factors in facilitating access to psychotropic medicines: a cross-sectional analysis of the WHO-AIMS in 63 Low- and middle-income countries. PLoS Med. 2012, 9 (1): e1001166-10.1371/journal.pmed.1001166.
2. Demyttenaere K, Bruffaerts R, Posada-Villa J, Gasquet I, Kovess V, Lepine JP, Angermeyer MC, Bernert S, de Girolamo G, Morosini P, et al: Prevalence, severity, and unmet need for treatment of mental disorders in the World Health Organization World Mental Health Surveys. JAMA. 2004, 291: 2581-2590.
3. Saraceno B, van Ommeren M, Batniji R, Cohen A, Gureje O, Mahoney J, Sridhar D, Underhill C: Barriers to improvement of mental health services in low-income and middle-income countries. Lancet. 2007, 370: 1164-1174. 10.1016/S0140-6736(07)61263-X.
4. Cohen A, Eaton J, Radtke B, George C, Manual BV, De Silva M, Patel V: Three models of community mental health services in low-income countries. International Journal of Mental Health Systems. 2011, 5: 1-10. 10.1186/1752-4458-5-1.
5. Patel V, Weiss HA, Chowdhary N, Naik S, Pednekar S, Chatterjee S, DeSilva MJ, Bhat B, Araya R, King M, et al: Effectiveness of an intervention led by lay heath counsellors for depressive and anxiety disorders in primary care in Goa, india (MANAS): a cluster randomized controlled trial. Lancet. 2010, 376: 2086-2095. 10.1016/S0140-6736(10)61508-5.
6. Araya R, Rojas G, Fritsch R, Gaete J, Rojas M, Simon G, Peters T: Treating depression in primary care in low-income women in Santiago, Chile: a randomised controlled trial. Lancet. 2003, 361: 995-1000. 10.1016/S0140-6736(03)12825-5.
7. Bolton P, Bass J, Neugebauer R, Verdeli H, Clougherty KF, Wickramaratne P, Speelman L, Ndogoni L, Weissman M: Group interpersonal psychotherapy for depression in rural Uganda: a randomized controlled trial. JAMA. 2003, 289 (23): 3117-3124. 10.1001/jama.289.23.3117.
8. Patel V, Thornicroft G: Packages of care for mental, neurological and substance use disorders in low- and middle-income countries: PLoS Medicine series. PLoS Med. 2009, 6: 1-2.
9. WHO: Mental Health Gap Action Programme: scaling up care for mental, neurological and substance use disorders. 2008, Geneva: WHO

10. Ventevogel P, van de Put W, Faiz H, van Mierlo B, Siddiqi M, Komproe IH: Improving access to mental health care and psychosocial support within a fragile context: a case study from Afghanistan. PLoS Med. 2012, 9 (5): 1-4.

11. Petersen I, Lund C, Bhana A, Flisher AJ, Consortium. tMHPRP: A task shifting approach to primary mental health care for adults in South Africa: human resource requirements and costs for rural settings. Health Policy Plan. 2012, 27 (1): 42-51. 10.1093/heapol/czr012.

12. Eaton J, Agomoh AO: Developing mental health services in Nigeria. Soc Psychiat Epidemiol. 2008, 43 (7): 552-558. 10.1007/s00127-008-0321-5.

13. Goncalves DA, Fortes S, Campos M, Ballester D, Portugal FB, Tófoli LF, Gask L, Mari J, Bower P: Evaluation of a mental health training intervention for multidisciplinary teams in primary care in Brazil: a pre-and posttest study. Gen Hosp Psychiatry. 2013, 35 (3): 304-308. 10.1016/j.genhosppsych.2013.01.003.

14. Acland S: Mental health services in primary care. World Mental Health Casebook: Social and Mental Programs in Low-Income Countries. Edited by: Cohen A, Kleinman A, Saraceno B. 2002, New York: Kluwer Academic/Plenum Publishers, 121-152.

15. Thornicroft G: Evidence-based mental health care and implementation science in low- and middle-income countries. Epidemiol Psychiatr Sci. 2012, 21: 241-244. 10.1017/ S2045796012000261.

16. Ventevogel P, Perez-Sales P, Fernandez-Liria A, Baingana F: Integrating mental health care into existing systems of health care: during and after complex humanitarian emergencies. Intervention. 2011, 9: 195-210.

17. Lund C, Tomlinson M, De Silva M, Fekadu A, Shidhaye R, Jordans MJD, Petersen I, Bhana A, Kigozi F, Prince M, et al: PRIME: a programme to reduce the treatment gap for mental disorders in five low- and middle-income countries. PLoS Med. 2012, 9 (12): e1001359-10.1371/journal.pmed.1001359.

18. Kohrt BA, Hruschka DJ, Worthman CM, Kunz RD, Baldwin JL, Upadhaya N, Acharya NR, Koirala S, Thapa SB, Tol WA, et al: Political violence and mental health in Nepal: prospective study. Br J Psychiatry. 2012, 2012: 268-275.

19. de Jong JTVM, Komproe IH, van Ommeren M: Common mental disorders in postconflict settings. Lancet. 2003, 361 (9375): 2128-2130. 10.1016/S0140-6736(03)13692-6.

20. Kruk ME, Freedman LP, Anglin GA, Waldman RJ: Rebuilding health systems to improve health and promote statebuilding in post-conflict countries: a theoretical framework and research agenda. Soc Sci Med. 2010, 70: 89-97. 10.1016/j. socscimed.2009.09.042.

21. Harmonized list of fragile situations. http://siteresources.worldbank.org/EXTLICUS/ Resources/511777-1269623894864/FCSHarmonizedListFY13.pdf,

22. Tol WA, Kohrt B, Jordans MJD, Thapa S, Pettigrew J, Upadhaya N, De Jong JTVM: Political violence and metal health: multi-disciplinary review of the literature on nepal. Soc Sci Med. 2009, DOI:10.1016/j.socsimed.2009.09.037

23. Anderson AA: Rhe Community Builder's Approach to Theory of Change: A Practical Guide to Theory Development. 2004, New York: The Aspen Institute, 1-37.

24. van Ommeren M, Sharma B, Thapa SB, Makaju R, Prasain D, Bhattarai R, de Jong JTVM: Preparing instruments for transcultural research: use of the translation monitoring form with Nepali-speaking Bhutanese refugees. Transcult Psychiatry. 1999, 36: 285-301. 10.1177/136346159903600304.

25. Rudan I, Gibson JL, Ameratunga S, El Arifeen S, Bhutta ZA, Black M, Black RE, Brown KH, Campbell H, Carneiro I, et al: Setting priorities in global child health

research investments: guidelines for implementation of CHNRI method. Croat Med J. 2008, 49 (6): 720-733. 10.3325/cmj.2008.49.720.

26. Lacey A, Luff D: Research and Development in Primary Health Care: An Introduction to Qualitative Analysis. 2001, Trent Focus

27. Patel V, Chowdhary N, Rahman A, Verdeli H: Improving access to psychological treatments: lessons from developing countries. Behav Res Ther. 2011, 49: 523-528. 10.1016/j.brat.2011.06.012.

28. Ventevogel P, Ndayisaba H, Van de Put W: Psychosocial assistance and decentralized mental health care in post conflict Burundi. Intervention. 2011, 9: 315-332.

29. Baingana F, Onyango Mangen P: Scaling up of mental health and trauma support among war-affected communities in northern Uganda: lessons learned. Intervention. 2011, 9: 291-303.

30. Hijazi Z, Weissbecker I, Chammay R: The integration of mental health into primary health care in Lebanon. Intervention. 2011, 9: 265-278.

31. Raja S, Underhill C, Shrestha P, Sunder U, Mannarath S, Kippen Wood S, Patel V: Integrating mental health and development: a case study of the BasicNeeds model in Nepal. PLoS Med. 2012, 9: e1001261-10.1371/journal.pmed.1001261.

Inequality Has Negative Impacts on Mental Health

Shoukai Yu

In the following excerpted viewpoint Shoukai Yu examines the correlation between social inequality and mental health. Gender inequality—factors such as domestic violence, lower wages, sexual abuse, and low social status—affects women's mental health across geographic and socio-economic strata. Wealth disparities also impact mental health for both women and men, although men are more apt to have depressive reactions to steep wealth inequality. The viewpoint concludes that more research needs to be conducted on a global level in order to address and treat mental health problems as a result of these inequalities. Shoukai Yu is a postdoctoral research fellow with the Harvard T.H. Chan School of Public Health.

As you read, consider the following questions:

1. Why is it important to study gender inequality's impact on mental health?
2. According to the viewpoint, what is the importance of studying inequality's impact on mental health from a global perspective?
3. How can this study's findings impact health policies around the world?

"Uncovering the Hidden Impacts of Inequality on Mental Health: A Global Study," by Shoukai Yu, Translational Psychiatry 8, Article number: 98 (2018), May 18, 2018. https://www.nature.com/articles/s41398-018-0148-0#Tab3. Licensed under CC BY 4.0 International.

According to the World Health Organization (WHO), depressive disorders are major contributors to the world's health burden; they affect approximately 350 million people worldwide.[1,2,3] Women are nearly twice as likely as men to suffer from mental illness.[4,5,6] Although this gender disparity in mental health is reported across diverse geographical regions, societies, populations, and social contexts, there is a dearth of research that explores a link between the impacts of social inequalities and gender disparities on mental health. In this study, the social inequalities include both gender inequality and wealth inequality. Understanding gender disparities in health is very important, according to the National Institutes of Health.[7,8,9,10] A growing body of research indicates that psychiatric disorders are largely caused by a combination of stress, environmental, neurobiological, and genetic factors. These poorly understood factors significantly limit the development of effective treatments for these disorders. The major causes for depressive disorders cannot be completely explained by genetic factors.[11,12,13] The contributions of genetic architectures are difficult to address at the level of health policy. Therefore, attention to social factors, especially with regard to inequality, is critical in approaches to mental health; these factors can be improved dramatically through the implementation of appropriate governmental policies and heightened community awareness.

The brain structure and response to stress are different between females and males.[14,15] For example, community pressure regarding stereotypical social roles based on gender may impact mental health responses differently in women and men.[16] In a male dominated culture, women and men may deal with competition in their workplaces differently. Previous studies also investigate the potential relationship between hegemonic masculinity and mental health in men.[17,18,19] Human genetic variation exists both within and among populations. These relevant genetic characteristics as well as stress could contribute to gender disparities in mental health.[20] The gender expectations and masculinities may also play an important role in gender disparities in mental health.[17,21,22] In a more general context, gender inequality includes but not limited to domestic violence, sexual abuse, unpaid caring work, higher hours of work, low social status, lack of access to reproductive rights and education.[23,24,25,26,27] Furthermore, the areas related to gender inequality include public health, social work, sociology, and social psychology.

Both gender inequality and wealth inequality have an impact on women's health at the country level.[26,28,29] For gender inequality research, a series of WHO reports provided in-depth reviews of available literature on the topic of gender equality and mental health in 2000.[30] Since then, there are some studies that have attempted to examine the association between gender inequality and gender disparity in mental health at the country level.[31,32] However, until now the evidence remains inconsistent for the possible impact of gender inequality on gender disparity in mental health.[31,32,33,34] In 2007, one study utilized the data from both high income and low and middle income countries and proved that gender equality has no or little impact on the gender disparities in depressive disorders.[32] In 2013, one study, based only on European countries, claimed the potential impact of gender equality on reducing the gender disparity in depressive disorders. Unfortunately, they were unable to provide statistical evidence to prove this association.[31] Therefore, at the global level, the direct statistical evidence to show the association between gender equality and the gender disparity in depressive disorders remains absent.

Wealth inequality has become a frequently and widely discussed topic.[31,35,36,37,38] Wealth inequality has impacted general health, including mental health.[39,40,41,42] Furthermore, the impact of wealth inequality on mental health has also been investigated.[43,44,45] Wealth inequality and income inequality are different: income represents the money received on a regular basis, while wealth represents the money or properties owed over a lifetime. However, research that attends to gender disparity in depressive disorders and the wealth inequality is limited.

This paper presented the statistical evidence to address this gap in the literature. The WHO has published a series of comprehensive reports about mental health[34,46,47] and has made a significant effort to collect the data that has permitted an exploration of the gender disparities in mental health.[29,30] The study in this paper captured the impact of social inequality on gender disparities in mental health. Previous studies that have not adequately addressed this problem typically analyzed the data using gender as a dichotomous variable. Moreover, the scope of many studies has been limited to specific countries.[24,48,49,50,51] For example, one study that indicated the potential correlation between the wage gap and gender disparities in mood disorders was limited to the United States and only used the wage gap to measure gender inequality.[24] Another study conducted only in South Korea also indicated that gender inequality might have an impact on mental health. In 2004, one study,[27] conducted in the United Kingdom, indicated domestic violence and abuse toward women related to the greater prevalence of mental illness among women. There is a need to utilize global datasets to identify the impact of inequality on mental health. Unlike existing studies, this study utilized mental health datasets at a global level to conduct the analysis; and the analyses in this study directly focused on the gender disparities on mental health. The novelty of the study in the paper lied in both data integration and the analysis. In order to illustrate the way that the present analysis can be used to better capture the relationships between mental health and inequality, this research also focused specifically on depressive disorders. All of the data were extracted from publicly available datasets and these data represent the largest sample size so far, due to the recent availability of global data on depressive disorders from the Global Burden of Disease database. The novelty analysis was straightforward: the ratio of depressive disorder rates for female to male is used directly as a dependent variable. In this way, gender disparity in depressive disorders can be modeled directly.

A series of statistical models were applied to examine the relationship between gender disparities in mental health and socioeconomic factors. Particular attention was paid to both gender and wealth inequalities. The study aimed to identify whether or not gender disparities in mental health are related to social inequalities, as well as to identify whether or not females respond differently to stress provoked by social inequality as evidenced in mental health outcomes. In this study, social inequality included both wealth inequality and gender inequality. The research was designed to inform public policy as well as to help health professionals reduce gender disparities in mental health and broadly improve mental health outcomes.

[…]

Discussion

This study demonstrated that social inequalities demonstrated a differential impact on mental health for females and males. For GII, greater gender inequality was significant and related to the decreased gender disparity in depressive disorders. This finding strongly suggested that women suffer mentally more than men in societies with greater levels of gender inequality. Combined with the significant correlation between RRFM and the GII index (1.043 [1.034, 1.053], P-value < 0.001), gender inequality had a significant impact on gender disparities in depressive disorders. This study provided evidence that social factors, especially gender inequalities may have significant impact on gender disparities in depressive disorders.

This study identified three major findings. First, gender inequality was significantly associated with increased gender disparities in depressive disorders. Previous studies that analyzed depressive disorders separately for females and males failed to detect the association between GII and mental disorder rates that was found here.[11] This study demonstrated that gender inequality may be associated with slightly higher DDRP for females. Moreover, gender inequality was associated with slightly lower DDRP for males. This study identified a significant association at the level of ratios, rather than at the level of rates. This distinction permitted an identification of the role that gender inequality played in depressive disorders.

[Regarding] the relationship between gender inequality and the mental health for female and male separately. For female, the estimate 0.039 [0.001, 0.081] is larger than 0, which indicates the greater gender inequality is related to the greater depression rate for women. While for male, the estimate −0.027 [−0.067, 0.013] is less than 0, which indicates the greater gender inequality is related to the lower depression rate for men. Both estimates do not reach the significance level for p values, while the P value for the ratio of female rates to male rates is significant. This is also one of the reasons why this association between gender inequality and mental health is hidden. Gender inequality includes but not limited to domestic violence, sexual abuse, unpaid caring work, higher hours of work, low social status, lack of access to reproductive rights and education.[23,24,25,26,27] The stress responses have been linked to depression.[43,64] In a male dominated culture, women and men may deal with competition in their workplaces differently. Previous studies also investigate the potential relationship between hegemonic masculinity and depressive disorders in men.[17,18,19]

Second, men suffered from more mental health problems than women when dealing with situations of high wealth inequality. This finding challenged assumptions that females would prove more emotionally or mentally sensitive to many social inequalities.[65,66] However, a high GINI index was significantly associated with high DDRP for males, whereas a high GINI index is not associated with high DDRP for females. This result is noteworthy and expands upon the contributions made by a recent study[24] that indicated that the wage gap may be related to higher rates of major depression for females in the United States. One possible explanation could be that males are more mentally sensitive to wealth inequality, due to either stress or their genetic makeup.[20,33,67,68] From a biological point of view, the presence of the Y chromosome and different hormones could also contribute to brain reactions to the wealth inequality. Yet, stereotypical social roles could put pressure on men to excel in the work place, producing greater levels of stress in men. This possibility would reaffirm the need to address inequality as an integral part of a plan to improve mental health among males. The higher GINI index was significantly associated with lower RRFM. However, the decreased gender disparity in depressive disorders was due to an increased DDRP for males, as opposed to a lower rate of depressive disorder rate among females.

Third, the GDP showed a direct association with RRFM, after adjusting for other socioeconomic factors and regional effects. Yet, the higher GDP correlate with slightly higher RRFM. Moreover, GDP did correlate with the prevalence of depressive disorders for both genders. This finding would suggest that higher overall wealth level for a country is not related to reducing gender disparity in depressive disorders. However, improving the overall level of wealth may indeed reduce the prevalence of depression in a specific population.[69,70,71]

In addition to this work's three major findings, there was one other finding that merits mention. Different geographical locations showed different regional impacts on gender disparities associated with depressive disorders. This finding was consistent with those from previous studies.[57,72,73] These results indicate that regional or geographical effects, as well as genetic factors (population differentiation, human genetic variation for different human populations), potentially played a role in gender disparities in depressive disorders. Regional and geographical variations could be due to the combination of effects of cultural, environmental, and socioeconomic factors.

There is substantial variability existed in GII index between countries. Similarly, there are also substantial variability existed in GINI index and GDP between countries. The high wealth inequality countries tend to cluster at Latin America and Caribbean, and some countries in the south part of Sub-Saharan Africa. The countries with higher GDP tend to have lower GINI index, such as Canada, the USA, Australia, and countries in Europe. Furthermore, there are some developing countries, such as China and some countries in the north part of Sub-Saharan Africa, although the GDP is not very high, the wealth inequality index is relatively low, which demonstrate the indirect correlation between GDP and GINI index. Overall, there is a cluster tendency for all of the three independent variables. Compared to the other two independent variables, the cluster tendency for GDP index is stronger.

Conclusion

This is one of the first studies to successfully provide statistical evidence of an association between gender disparities in psychiatric disorders and social inequalities at a global level. These results contribute to the growing evidence that social inequality has an independent effect on population-specific depressive disorders.[24,48] This study was enhanced by a multi-faceted approach to the matter of inequality that utilized both the United Nations' definition of inequality and measures of inequality such that gender inequality could be captured more precisely. The novelty in the paper lied in the analysis using existing databases. The overall results suggested that diverse aspects of social inequality, including both gender inequality and wealth inequality, evidenced differential impacts on mental health for both genders.

Caution should be exercised in interpreting and extrapolating the study results to posit broader generalizations regarding mental health. The study results only demonstrated correlations rather than causal links between inequality and depressive disorders. A focus on causal relationships between policies, such as economic, education and public health and mental health may not adequately capture the complexity of social interactions and the nature of mental disorders. The causal relationship could be further explored from the genomics and etiology aspects. Moreover, this study analyzed gender inequality and wealth inequality at the country level, and there is no apparent correlation between GII and GINI indexes.

If future analysis is utilized for research on a local scale, such as at the level of community or county, the correlation between gender inequality and wealth inequality should be taken into account in the modeling process. Furthermore, attention should be drawn to the potential collinearity between the independent variables. Additionally, this study was based solely on the genders recorded in the GBD database (female, male, and both combined), with no information on lesbian, gay, bisexual, and transgender populations.

Improvement in a given population's mental health would require a multidisciplinary policy approach that addresses socioeconomic determinants of health. Wealth inequality has become a pressing issue in a wide range of countries internationally.[23,74,75,76] Moreover, many researchers have shown that socioeconomic status has impacted general health.[39,40,41,42] Recently, many studies have focused on the gender differences regarding health.[77,78,79,80] Unlike most previous studies on inequality and health, this research specifically demonstrated the association between the effects of socioeconomic inequality gender disparities on mental health. Future research could further explore the causal relationships that might exist between social factors and mental health outcomes. Currently, the global burden of disease database lack country level data for mental health for majority countries81. The data at the country level for the global burden of disease study could further improve our understanding the association between socioeconomic determinants and mental health.

The findings presented here provided strong evidence of a relationship between high gender inequality and a higher ratio of depressive disorder rates for both females and males. This significant correlation might be partially explained by gender discrimination. Gender prejudice, either overt or covert, could subject females to the experience of greater barriers to accessing community resources, including mental health care, that contribute to better health. The regions that exhibited high rates of common mental disorders also exhibited high levels of inequality, as reported by the WHO.[6] The United Nations emphasized the need for increased attention to factors that link gender disparities to health, including education, inclusion in policy decisions, participation, income, and differential socioeconomic status in its 17 sustainable development goals. It would be important to focus on the impact of policies designed to further equality, including both gender equality and wealth equality, in order to address existing mental health disparities and achieve the highest possible level of health for all people.

Endnotes

1. Marcus, M., Yasamy, M. T., van Ommeren, M., Chisholm, D. & Saxena, S. Depression: a global public health concern Vol. 1. WHO Department of Mental Health and Substance Abuse 6–8 (2012).
2. López, A. D. & Murray, C. J. The Global Burden of Disease: A Comprehensive Assesment of Mortality and Disability from Diseases, Injuries, and Risk Factors in 1990 and Projected to 2020 (Harvard School of Public of Public Health, 1996).
3. National Institutes of Health. The Numbers Count: Mental Disorders in America (NIH Publication no. 01-4584) (National Institutes of Health, Bethesda, 2014).
4. Weissman, M. M. & Olfson, M. Depression in women: implications for health care research. Science 269, 799 (1995).
5. Desai, H. D. & Jann, M. W. Major depression in women: a review of the literature. J. Am. Pharm. Assoc. 40, 525–537 (1999).
6. World Health Organization Department of Mental Health and Substance Dependence. Gender Disparities in Mental Health (World Health Organization, Geneva, 2013).
7. Doyal, L. Sex, gender, and health: the need for a new approach. Br. Med. J. 323, 1061 (2001).
8. Pinn, V. W. Sex and gender factors in medical studies: implications for health and clinical practice. JAMA 289, 397–400 (2003).
9. Vlassoff, C. Gender differences in determinants and consequences of health and illness. J. Health Popul. Nutr. 25, 47–61 (2007).
10. Gahagan, J., Gray, K. & Whynacht, A. Sex and gender matter in health research: addressing health inequities in health research reporting. Int. J. Equity Health 14, 1 (2015).
11. Sanders, A. R., Detera-Wadleigh, S. D., & Gershon, E. S. Molecular genetics of mood disorders. In: Charney DDS, Nestler EJ, Bunney ES, eds. Neurobiology of Mental Illness. 1st ed. New York: Oxford; 1999:299-316.
12. Sullivan, P. F., Neale, M. C. & Kendler, K. S. Genetic epidemiology of major depression: review and meta-analysis. Am. J. Psychiatry 157, 1552–1562 (2000).
13. Fava, M. & Kendler, K. S. Major depressive disorder. Neuron 28, 335–341 (2000).
14. Canli, T., Desmond, J. E., Zhao, Z. & Gabrieli, J. D. Sex differences in the neural basis of emotional memories. Proc. Natl Acad. Sci. USA 99, 10789–10794 (2002).
15. Ruigrok, A. N. et al. A meta-analysis of sex differences in human brain structure. Neurosci. Biobehav. Rev. 39, 34–50 (2014).
16. Eagly, A. H. & Wood, W. The origins of sex differences in human behavior: evolved dispositions versus social roles. Am. Psychol. 54, 408 (1999).

17. Courtenay, W. H. Constructions of masculinity and their influence on men's well-being: a theory of gender and health. Soc. Sci. Med. 50, 1385–1401 (2000).

18. Evans, J., Frank, B., Oliffe, J. L. & Gregory, D. Health, illness, men and masculinities (HIMM): a theoretical framework for understanding men and their health. J. Men's Health 8, 7–15 (2011).

19. Emslie, C., Ridge, D., Ziebland, S. & Hunt, K. Men's accounts of depression: reconstructing or resisting hegemonic masculinity? Soc. Sci. Med. 62, 2246–2257 (2006).

20. Goldstein, J. M., Jerram, M., Abbs, B., Whitfield-Gabrieli, S. & Makris, N. Sex differences in stress response circuitry activation dependent on female hormonal cycle. J. Neurosci. 30, 431–438 (2010).

21. Chua, P. & Fujino, D. C. Negotiating new Asian-American masculinities: attitudes and gender expectations. J. Men's Stud. 7, 391–413 (1999).

22. Pleck, J. H. The gender role strain paradigm: an update. In: Levant RF, Pollack WS. eds. A New Psychology of Men, New York: Basic Books, 11–32 (1995).

23. Maume, D. J. & Ruppanner, L. State liberalism, female supervisors, and the gender wage gap. Soc. Sci. Res. 50, 126–138 (2015).

24. Platt, J., Prins, S., Bates, L. & Keyes, K. Unequal depression for equal work? How the wage gap explains gendered disparities in mood disorders. Soc. Sci. Med. 149, 1–8 (2016).

25. Orloff, A. S. Gender and the social rights of citizenship: the comparative analysis of gender relations and welfare states. Am. Sociol. Rev. 58, 303–328 (1993).

26. Moss, N. E. Gender equity and socioeconomic inequality: a framework for the patterning of women's health. Soc. Sci. Med. 54, 649–661 (2002).

27. Walby, S., Allen, J., Simmons, J. Domestic Violence, Sexual Assault and Stalking: Findings from the British Crime Survey (Home Office Research, Development and Statistics Directorate, London, 2004).

28. Borrell, C. et al. Influence of macrosocial policies on women's health and gender inequalities in health. Epidemiol. Rev. 36, 31–48 (2014).

29. World Health Organization. Gender Differences in the Epidemiology of Affective Disorders and Schizophrenia (World Health Organization, Geneva, 1997).

30. World Health Organization. Women's Mental Health: An Evidence Based Review (World Health Organization, Geneva, 2000).

31. Van de Velde, S., Huijts, T., Bracke, P. & Bambra, C. Macro-level gender equality and depression in men and women in Europe. Sociol. Health Illn. 35, 682–698 (2013).

32. Hopcroft, R. L. & Bradley, D. B. The sex difference in depression across 29 countries. Social. Forces 85, 1483–1507 (2007).

33. Hagen, E. H. & Rosenström, T. Explaining the sex difference in depression with a unified bargaining model of anger and depression. Evol. Med. Public Health 2016, 117–132 (2016).

34. Seedat, S. et al. Cross-national associations between gender and mental disorders in the World Health Organization World Mental Health Surveys. Arch. Gen. Psychiatry 66, 785–795 (2009).

35. Reiss, F. Socioeconomic inequalities and mental health problems in children and adolescents: a systematic review. Soc. Sci. Med. 90, 24–31 (2013).

36. Marmot, M. & Bell, R. Fair society, healthy lives. Public. Health 126, S4–S10 (2012).

37. Wilkinson, R. & Pickett, K. The Spirit Level: Why Equality is Better for Everyone (Penguin UK, 2010).

38. Black, R. E. et al. Maternal and child undernutrition and overweight in low-income and middle-income countries. Lancet 382, 427–451 (2013).

39. Eckersley, R. Beyond inequality: acknowledging the complexity of social determinants of health. Soc. Sci. Med. 147, 121–125 (2015).

40. Foverskov, E. & Holm, A. Socioeconomic inequality in health in the British household panel: tests of the social causation, health selection and the indirect selection hypothesis using dynamic fixed effects panel models. Soc. Sci. Med. 150, 172–183 (2016).

41. Undurraga, E. A., Behrman, J. R., Leonard, W. R. & Godoy, R. A. The effects of community income inequality on health: evidence from a randomized control trial in the Bolivian Amazon. Soc. Sci. Med. 149, 66–75 (2016).

42. Bhargava, A., Jamison, D. T., Lau, L. J. & Murray, C. J. Modeling the effects of health on economic growth. J. Health Econ. 20, 423–440 (2001).

43. Pickett, K. E. & Wilkinson, R. G. Inequality: an underacknowledged source of mental illness and distress. Br. J. Psychiatry 197, 426–428 (2010).

44. Murali, V. & Oyebode, F. Poverty, social inequality and mental health. Adv. Psychiatr. Treat. 10, 216–224 (2004).

45. Ramon, S. Inequality in mental health: The relevance of current research and understanding to potentially effective social work responses. Radic. Psychol. 6, 1–23 (2007).

46. World Health Organization. Mental health: responding to the call for action, report by the Secretariat Vol. 55. 55th World Health Assembly A (World Health Organization, Geneva, 2002).

47. World Health Organization. Mental health action plan 2013–2020. (2013) http://www.who.int/mental_health/publications/action_plan/en/.

48. Gitto, L., Noh, Y.-H. & Andrés, A. R. An Instrumental Variable Probit (IVP) analysis on depressed mood in Korea: the impact of gender differences and other socioeconomic factors. Int. J. Health Policy Manag. 4, 523 (2015).

49. Seguino, S. Gender inequality and economic growth: a cross-country analysis. World Dev. 28, 1211–1230 (2000).

50. Bhan, N., Rao, K. D. & Kachwaha, S. Health inequalities research in India: a review of trends and themes in the literature since the 1990s. Int. J. Equity Health 15, 166 (2016).

51. Cheng, H. G. et al. Social correlates of mental, neurological, and substance use disorders in China and India: a review. Lancet Psychiatry 3, 882–899 (2016).

64. Wada, K. et al. Relationship between the onset of depression and stress response measured by the Brief Job Stress Questionnaire among Japanese employees: a cohort study. PLoS ONE 8, e56319 (2013).

65. Grossman, M. & Wood, W. Sex differences in intensity of emotional experience: a social role interpretation. J. Pers. Soc. Psychol. 65, 1010 (1993).

66. Lungu, O., Potvin, S., Tikàsz, A. & Mendrek, A. Sex differences in effective fronto-limbic connectivity during negative emotion processing. Psychoneuroendocrinology 62, 180–188 (2015).

67. Naninck, E., Lucassen, P. & Bakker, J. Sex differences in adolescent depression: do sex hormones determine vulnerability? J. Neuroendocrinol. 23, 383–392 (2011).

68. Parker, G. & Brotchie, H. Gender differences in depression. Int. Rev. Psychiatry 22, 429–436 (2010).

69. Muntaner, C., Eaton, W., Diala, C., Kessler, R. & Sorlie, P. Social class, assets, organizational control and the prevalence of common groups of psychiatric disorders. Soc. Sci. Med. 47, 2043–2053 (1998).

70. Pollack, C. E. et al. Should health studies measure wealth?: a systematic review. Am. J. Prev. Med. 33, 250–264 (2007).

71. Carter, K. N., Blakely, T., Collings, S., Gunasekara, F. I. & Richardson, K. What is the association between wealth and mental health? J. Epidemiol. Community Health 63, 221–226 (2009).

72. Ferrari, A. J. et al. The burden attributable to mental and substance use disorders as risk factors for suicide: findings from the Global Burden of Disease Study 2010. PLoS ONE 9, e91936 (2014).

73. Lopez, A. D., Mathers, C. D., Ezzati, M., Jamison, D. T. & Murray, C. J. Global and regional burden of disease and risk factors, 2001: systematic analysis of population health data. Lancet 367, 1747–1757 (2006).

74. McGee, A., McGee, P. & Pan, J. Performance pay, competitiveness, and the gender wage gap: evidence from the United States. Econ. Lett. 128, 35–38 (2015).

75. Guimarães, CRFF. & Silva, JR. Pay gap by gender in the tourism industry of Brazil. Tour. Manag. 52, 440–450 (2016).

76. Mandel, H. The role of occupational attributes in gender earnings inequality, 1970–2010. Soc. Sci. Res. 55, 122–138 (2016).

77. Jagger, C. et al. Inequalities in healthy life years in the 25 countries of the European Union in 2005: a cross-national meta-regression analysis. Lancet 372, 2124–2131 (2009).

78. Oksuzyan, A., Shkolnikova, M., Vaupel, J., Christensen, K. & Shkolnikov, V. Sex differences in health and mortality in Moscow and Denmark. Eur. J. Epidemiol. 29, 243–252 (2014).

79. World Health Organization. Ageing and Life Course, Family and Community Health: WHO Global Report on Falls Prevention in Older Age (World Health Organization, Geneva, 2008).

80. Nusselder, W., Looman, C., Oyen, H., Robine, J.-M. & Jagger, C. Gender differences in health of EU10 and EU15 populations: the double burden of EU10 men. Eur. J. Ageing 7, 219–227 (2010).

81. Whiteford, H., Ferrari, A. & Degenhardt, L. Global burden of disease studies: implications for mental and substance use disorders. Health Aff. 35, 1114–1120 (2016).

In India Mental Illness Is a Ticking Time Bomb

Moin Qazi

In the following viewpoint, Moin Qazi details the looming mental health crisis faced in India. Called India's ticking time bomb, Ram Nath Kovind, President of the National Institute of Mental Health and Neurosciences, stated that the country is potentially facing an epidemic. According to the World Health Organization (WHO), 6.5 percent of India's population suffers from mental illness, and without acknowledgement that number could grow as high as 20 percent by 2020. With only 3,800 psychiatrists and almost 900 clinical psychologists practicing in India, there are significant gaps in a person's ability to seek treatment, especially those who do not live in urban areas. Moin Qazi is the author of the bestselling book, Village Diary of a Heretic Banker. *He has worked in the development finance sector for almost four decades.*

"India's Grey Clouds of Depression," by Moin Qazi, The Asian Age, April 16, 2018. Reprinted by permission.

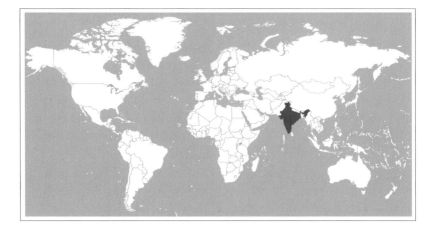

As you read, consider the following questions:

1. According to the viewpoint, how significant is the number of people suffering from mental illness in India?
2. Considering India's population of approximately 1.339 billion, how significant is it that 3 percent of the population suffers from anxiety disorders?
3. What is more significant, the state of mental healthcare in India or government apathy regarding mental health treatment?

Among the many challenges India faces, the most underappreciated is the ongoing mental health crisis. Mental illness is actually India's ticking bomb. An estimated 56 million Indians suffer from depression, and 38 million from anxiety disorders. For those who suffer from mental illness, life can seem like a terrible prison from which there is no hope of escape; they are left forlorn and abandoned, stigmatized, shunned and misunderstood.

The intensity of mental disorders is particularly worrying in the adolescents. Half of all mental illness starts by the age of 14, but most cases go undetected and untreated. Suicide is the second leading cause of death among 15- 29-year-olds.

The pathetic state of mental health care in the country coupled with government's apathy is a cause of great concern. A plausible reason is the sheer scale of the problem. Hence, nobody wants to discuss the elephant in the room. However, the nation cannot afford to ignore the stark reality. There are only about 43 mental hospitals in the country, and most of them are in disarray. Six states, mainly in the northern and eastern regions with a combined population of 56 million people, do not have a single mental hospital. Most government–run mental hospitals lack essential infrastructure, treatment facilities and have a sickening ambience. Visiting private clinics and sustaining the treatment, which is usually a long, drawn-out affair, is an expensive proposition for most families.

According to a Ministry of Health and Family Welfare report, India faces a treatment gap of 50-70 percent for mental health care. The government data highlights the dismal number of mental healthcare professionals in India; 3,800 psychiatrists and just 898 clinical psychologists. A large number of them are situated in urban areas. The WHO reports that there are only three psychiatrists per million people in India, while in other Commonwealth countries, the ratio is 5.6 psychiatrists for the same. By this estimate, India is short of 66,200 psychiatrists.

Mental health care accounts for 0.16 percent of the total Union Health Budget, which is less than that of Bangladesh, which spends 0.44 percent. A developed nation's expenditure on the same amounts to an average of 4 percent. India must find better ways to parlay its impressive economic growth into faster progress in this critical area as maintaining an ignorant stance on the issue will not help in its resolve.

A survey conducted by the All India Institute of Medical Sciences (AIIMS) in collaboration with WHO across 11 centres in the country, involving 3,000 people from each city found that 95 percent of those with mental-health problems remain deprived of treatment due to stigma, shame and getting shunned from societies. Three age groups are particularly vulnerable to depression: pregnant or post-partum women, the youth and the elderly.

With resources tight, an effective method for successfully tackling mental illness is a major expansion of online psychiatric resources such as virtual clinics and web-based psychotherapies. The economic consequences of poor mental health are quite significant. The cognitive symptoms of depression, like difficulties in concentrating, making decisions and remembering, cause significant impairment in work function and productivity. A World Economic Forum-Harvard School of Public Health study estimated that the cumulative global impact of mental disorders in terms of lost economic output will amount to $16.3 trillion between 2011 and 2030. In India, mental illness is estimated to cost $1.03 trillion (22 percent of the economic output) during 2012-2030. Estimates suggest that by 2025, 38.1m years of healthy life will be lost to mental illness in India (23% increase).

The fact is that poor mental health is just as bad as or maybe even worse than any kind of physical injury. Left untreated, it can lead to debilitating, life-altering conditions. Medical science has progressed enough to be able to cure, or at least control, nearly all of the mental-health problems with a combination of drugs, therapy and community support. Individuals can lead fulfilling and productive lives while performing day-to-day activities such as going to school, raising a family and pursuing a career.

Although mental illness is experienced by a significant portion of the population, it is still seen as a taboo. Depression is so deeply stigmatised that people adopt enforced silence and social isolation. In villages, there are dreadful, recorded cases of patients being locked up in homes during the day, being tied to trees or even being flogged to exorcise evil spirits. Stories of extreme barbarity abound in tribal cultures. In some societies, family honour is so paramount that the notion of seeking psychiatric help more regularly is considered to be anathema to them. Recognition and acknowledgement, rather than denial and ignorance are the need of the hour.

Many a time, mental-health problems are either looked down upon or trivialised. These man-made barriers deprive people of their dignity. We need to shift the paradigm of how we view and address mental illness at a systemic level. Tragically, support networks for the mentally ill are woefully inadequate. There is an urgent need for an ambience of empathy, awareness and acceptance of these people so that prejudices dissipate and patients are able to overcome the stigma and shame.

India's Mental Health Care Act is a very progressive legislation, and is the equivalent of a bill of rights for people with mental disorders. Fundamentally, the Act treats mental disorders on the same plane as physical health problems thus stripping it of all stigmatizations. Mental health issues get the same priority as physical disorders. Conceptually, it transforms the focus of mental health legislations from supposedly protecting society and families by relegating people with mental disorders to second-class citizens, to emphasizing the provision of affordable and quality care, financed by the government, through the primary care system.

There have been some encouraging innovations in India, led by voluntary organisations that are both impactful and replicable. Dr Vikram Patel, who is a professor at the London School of Hygiene and Tropical Medicine and co-founder of the Goa-based mental health research non-profit "Sangath," has been at the forefront of community mental health programmes in central India.

It deploys health workers, some with no background in mental health. The mission tasks community-based workers to provide low intensity psychosocial interventions and raise mental health awareness and provide "psychological first-aid." Since they are drawn from the same community, they are able to empathise with the patients. The next stage consists of mental health professionals. The programme uses Primary Health Centres for screening people with mental illnesses.

According to Patel, mental-health support workers can be trained at a modest cost. Given the limited availability of mental-health professionals, such first-aid approaches can be suitably and successfully adapted to community needs with limited resources. The senior therapists can be given basic training in general

---

Mental Health Disorders in Indonesia

Mental health disorders are often hidden from view. People often think of mental disorders with images of a naked homeless person in the street. But there is a wide spectrum of these problems.

There is a stigma around mental health problems. Among the general public this ranges from stereotyping and prejudice to discrimination against people with mental illness. People with mental health problems are often considered dangerous, possessed by demons or affected by black magic.

The resulting fears lead to the belief that they should be kept away from the communities. Consequently, in 2017, 28.1% of people with mental illness were still locked in or shackled in or around their house. Self stigma turns the sufferers against themselves, hindering them and their family from seeking help early and therefore preventing them from receiving proper treatment and care.

Victims of disasters are also very prone to mental health problems. With Indonesia being located in a region with high risks of earthquakes, tsunami and volcanic eruptions, a lot of people have been affected by disasters. They need psychological support to go through the difficult times of losing their loved ones, their belongings and the fear of future disasters.

---

medicine, psychology, psychiatry, psychopharmacology, social work and patient management.

His model envisages the involvement of primary care—based counsellors and community-based workers to reduce the burden of depression in the population. There is no longer any doubt about whether community health workers can be trained and supervised to deliver clinically effective psychosocial interventions. The challenge before us now is how to go beyond pilots and research studies and scale these innovations up in routine health care. Involvement of the social, health and education sectors in comprehensive, integrated, evidence-based programmes for the mental health of young people is vital for strneghtening the overall healthcare framework at the grassroots level.

Another mental health issue, rarely addressed in Indonesia, is peripartum depression, occurring during pregnancy and after delivery. The World Health Organisation (WHO) reports that in developing nations 15.6% of pregnant women and 19.8% of lactating women experience this condition.

Not only can depression lead to suicides but it also reduces mothers' ability to care for their children. Given that the country is focusing on efforts to reduce stunting, detecting peripartum depression and helping mothers seek treatment can help them raise healthy and smart children.

Mental health problems occur in people of all ages. Mental disorders are prevalent among youth, as this is the time when people face many different transitions in life. The WHO 2018 World Mental Health Day (October 10) recognised this by making this year's theme "Young People and Mental Health in The Changing World".

But mental problems also affect the middle-aged population. A national survey in 2013 showed that the proportion of mental and emotional problems increased with age. The problems are also common among the poor.

"260 million People and Less Than 1000 Psychiatrists, Indonesia's Mental Health Worker Shortage," by Susy K. Sebayang, Marty Mawarpury and Rizanna Rosemary, The Conversation, November 2, 2018.

Mental healthcare initiatives are presently focused on a narrow biomedical approach that tends to ignore socio-cultural contexts. Community mental-health services can offer a mix of clinical, psychological and social services to people with severe, moderate and mild mental illnesses. Also, counselling can make a profound difference and build resilience to cope with despair. Providing psychoeducation to the patients' families can also help. Unfortunately, in recent decades, academic psychologists have largely forsaken psychoanalysis and made themselves over as biologists. There is need for strengthening the cadre of behavioral health therapists.

Prevention must begin with people being made aware of the early warning signs and symptoms of mental illness. Parents and teachers can help build life skills of children and adolescents to help them cope with everyday challenges at home and at school. Psychosocial support can be provided in schools and other community settings. Training for health workers to enable them to detect and manage mental health disorders can be put in place, improved or expanded. Such programmes should also cover peers, parents and teachers so that they know how to support their friends, children and students overcome mental stress and neurotic problems. There is a need for more open discussion and dialogue on this subject with the general public, and not just experts. This can help create a more inclusive environment for people with mental illness.

Lewis Carroll very succinctly summed up the plight of today's human beings in the conversation between the Queen and Alice in his classic *Alice in Wonderland*. Here's the paraphrase: Alice tells the queen that one has to run at the top of one's speed to excel in a competitive race. The queen disagrees and we see the essence of competitive existence when she tells Alice that in her country one has to do all the running at the top most speed to retain one's position. But if you want to get somewhere you have to run twice as fast. This is the paradox. Everyone wants to go somewhere. But they don't know where. This is the reason for the growing incidence of depression in society.

With simple yet effective steps, we can turn the situation around and build a more accommodating environment for those struggling with mental distress.

In the United Kingdom Work Can Make You Mentally Ill

Chris O'Sullivan

In the following excerpted viewpoint, Chris O'Sullivan covers the relationship between work and mental health, and how it is becoming more and more of a priority for both policy makers and employers. With an emphasis on prevention, the viewpoint details the research, which focuses on the relationships between work and common mental health problems, including the twelve work-related risk factors identified in numerous research studies. Among the studies, it shows that increased workload and time pressure creates high-stress situations that are associated with an increased risk of illness and reduced wellbeing. Chris O'Sullivan works for the Mental Health Foundation, a national mental health charity focused on prevention in mental health, with an interest in promoting mental health at work.

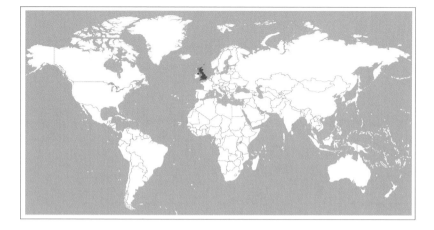

As you read, consider the following questions:

1. Per the viewpoint, how much money can potentially be saved if people in the United Kingdom were able to receive treatment for mental health?

2. What are ways in which a company or organization can support the mental health of its employees?

3. Is there a relationship between job insecurity and poor mental health? Why or why not?

The relationship between work and mental health is becoming a priority both for policy makers and employers. We know that when our workplaces support our ability to thrive, the identity, income and purpose that work can bring can be good for our mental health. Equally, much has been written about the impact of toxic working environments in terms of the impact of bullying, harassment and discrimination at work.

To date, much of the focus of debate has been on the cost of lost productivity due to mental ill health; of the order of £26 billion per year. According to recent research using Labour Force Survey data (Mental Health Foundation, 2016), the value added by people in the UK working with mental health problems is as many as nine time greater at £226 billion per year, or 12.1% of total GDP (gross domestic produce).

We need to know more about how to protect and improve mental health as a workplace asset. Prevention is a major focus of interest in workplace mental health going forward, but the evidence for interventions are in their infancy, a topic covered by Laurence Palfreyman in a Mental Elf blog in June 2014.

Methods

The authors adopted a robust search strategy for English language reviews using MEDLINE, PsychInfo, Embase and the Cochrane Collaboration databases. The review included only papers that considered common mental health problems, specifically depression, anxiety and/or work related stress, in which the role of work or work related risk factors were considered.

The quality of selected reviews was assessed using the AMSTAR checklist, with the quality of reviews presented throughout the findings, emphasising evidence that came from reviews with moderate or high quality scores.

Results

A wealth of evidence supporting a relationship between work and common mental health problems.

From an initial search screen of 7,542 studies, 40 full texts were screened and 37 reviews were found to meet the inclusion criteria. Of these, seven reviews scored as being of at least moderate quality on AMSTAR. These seven included analysed 213 primary research studies, with evidence of only minimal overlap between studies included. Twelve work related risk factors were identified amongst the included reviews. These factors were assessed in relation to a number of existing models for framing stress and distress in the workplace.

Summary of Evidence Relating to Established Models of Workplace Mental Health

Job Demand-Control-Support (JDCS) Model

Asserts that jobs where low control over factors such as decision making are combined with high demands, such as increased workload/time pressure created a 'high strain' situation and can be associated with the highest risk of illness and reduced wellbeing.

Some evidence suggests that good social support in the workplace may moderate these adverse effects (Sanne, Mykletun, Dahl et al, 2005).

Good evidence for a relationship between poorer employee mental health and high job demand, low job control and low social support.

Stansfield and Candy (2006) found that the risk of an employee developing a common mental health problem could be predicted by low job control, high psychological demands and low occupational social support.

Theorell et al (2015), Nieuwenhuijsen et al (2010) and Netterstrom et al (2008) found a connection between these factors and the development of depression, and the occurrence of stress related disorders.

Effort Reward Imbalance (ERI) Model

Based on an employee's perception of the balance between the effort they put into their work and the reward (financial and otherwise) they received for this. It proposes that the most stressful situations are those where the reward is lower than the effort (Siergrist, Stark, Chadola et al, 2004).

Three reviews of moderate quality explored the impact of high ERI on the mental health of workers.

Stansfield and Candy (2006) concluded that High ERI is associated with increased risk of common mental disorders; based on comparison of two longitudinal studies with over 12,000 subjects.

Nieuwenhuijsen et al (2010) found a significant association between high ERI and stress related disorders on the workplace.

Theorell et al (2015) identified some limited evidence for a relationship between high ERI and increased depression symptoms.

Organisational Justice Model

The organisational justice model (Elovainio et al, 2002) refers to the fairness of rules and social norms within companies in three dimensions:

- The distribution of resources and benefits (Distributive Justice)

- The methods and processes governing that distribution (Procedural Justice)

- Interpersonal relationships (Interactional Justice), which includes two elements:

  - The level of dignity and respect received from management (Relational Justice)

  - The presence or absence of adequate information from management about workplace procedures (Informational Justice)

Two moderate quality and one low quality review explored this relationship, with most studies focusing on relational and procedural justice.

Nieuwenhuijsen et al (2010) found that low relational justice and low procedural justice were associated with increased risk of stress related disorders

Theorell et al (2015) found more limited evidence for the impact on either procedural or relational justice on depression symptoms

One lower quality review (Ndjaboue et al, 2012) found that low procedural justice and low relational justice were associated with increased likelihood of mental health problems amongst employees.

Additional Factors Considered

Organisational Change and Job Security

Organisational change is now a given in working life in most fields. Bamberger et al (2012) reviewed 17 studies assessing various forms of organisational change. Eleven of these studies observed a negative relationship between organisational change and mental health.

There is some evidence for a relationship between job insecurity and poor mental health with one review of three studies reporting a moderate odds ratio between the factors (Stansfield and Candy, 2006). In contrast Theorell et al (2015) concluded that there was only limited evidence for an association between job insecurity and depression symptoms.

Employment Status and Atypical Working Hours

Virtanen et al (2005) reported that temporary employees have higher psychological morbidity compared with permanent employees. Harvey et al point out though that the definition of psychological morbidity is not clear, and also reflect that many people with mental health problems are more likely to be offered temporary contracts compared with 'healthy individuals'.

In terms of working hours, the review points mainly to the impact of long working hours. Theorell et al (2015) show limited evidence of an association between a 'long working week' and depressive symptoms.

Workplace Conflict and Bullying

The authors identified five meta-analyses that examined the impact of workplace conflict and bullying on the development of mental disorders.

Theorell et al (2015) showed moderately strong evidence for an association between workplace bullying and increased depression symptoms. In the same review, there was only limited evidence for an impact of workplace conflict with superiors and co-workers on depression symptoms. Verkuil et al (2015) showed that workplace bullying increased symptoms of depression, anxiety and stress related psychological symptoms, although there were some questions raised about the quality of this review.

Role stress

The two most researched aspects of role stress in relation to mental health are:

- Role ambiguity: where an employee lacks information about their role's responsibilities and objectives

- Role conflict: when there are two or more opposing expectations about the employee's role.

One meta-analysis of 32 studies (Schmidt et al, 2014) analysed by the authors found that role conflict and role ambiguity were related to an increase in depressive symptoms.

Conclusions

A new model for linking and understanding potential risk factors in the workplace.

Based on the findings of the review, the authors present a new, unifying model of the psychosocial workplace with three overlapping clusters of workplace risk factors; imbalanced job design, occupational uncertainty and a lack of value and respect within the workplace.

Subject to the limitations discussed below and identified by the team, the review suggests four conclusions regarding the relationship between work and common mental disorders:

1. There is consistent evidence for an association between some workplace situations and common mental health problems, though methodological concerns mean casual inferences must be made with caution

2. There are a further range of emerging work factors that appear to increase the risk of common mental health problems, but where further research is needed

3. There is no magic bullet or single source of toxicity, but there are new overlaps between factors emerging

4. The interaction between individual and organisational factors is complicated, and there is a need for better methodologies to assess the direction of causality.

Strengths and Limitations

A strong meta-review, with some reservations about methodological weaknesses in some of the included studies.

It is perhaps a surprise that efforts to bring together themes relating to risk factors for common mental health problems in the workplace has not been done before. The authors appear to have produced a robust, valuable review that uses a strong methodology, and errs on the side of caution in both inclusion criteria and in anticipating potential concerns in reporting and limitations of the study.

As the team point out, meta-review methodologies allow coverage of a wide range of themes, and this has certainly been the case here, drawing together evidence on twelve separate potential risk factors. The down side, as identified, is that the time taken for reviews to be published can lead to primary research of potential conclusion altering relevance not being included in a 'definitive' meta-review.

There are key areas in the model proposed where the pace of change in workplace contexts is such that there are gaps which could and should be filled. Most notably these could include studies relating to insecure employment in zero-hours contracts or other precarious employment.

There are some key limitations in the body of primary research that are picked up by the authors and are worthy of further consideration.

Firstly the authors point to the challenges of using self-reporting questionnaires to source data from employees about their experiences both of distress, and of circumstances relating to their employment. It is possible that a wide range of personal beliefs, attitudes and individual factors will influence respondents' ability to accurately comment on their experience.

The authors also point to the possibility of reverse causation being a factor:

> Reverse causation is also a possibility via early life mental illness increasing the risk of an individual finding themselves working in a suboptimal environment.

People with life history of mental health problems are still subject to profound inequalities, including in accessing and thriving in the labour market. If we are to address the very real challenges of ensuring work environments support people with declared and undeclared lived experience, we must see both sides of this equation; understanding not just how working life affects the development of mental health problems, but also how these same competing pressures interact with existing mental health concerns and personal factors such as experience of trauma. Research looking at mental health and the workplace must pay due regard to this complexity, and we must seek methodologies that enable robustness and replicability, without becoming too in-vitro and artificial.

[...]

Periodical and Internet Sources Bibliography

The following articles have been selected to supplement the diverse views presented in this chapter.

Amnesty International, "Syria: Unlawful attacks by government forces hit civilians and medical facilities in Idlib," Amnesty International, March 28, 2019. https://www.amnesty.org/en/latest/news/2019/03/syria-unlawful-attacks-by-government-forces-hit-civilians-and-medical-facilities-in-idlib/.

BBC News, "Syria war: Hospitals being targeted, aid workers say," BBC News, January 6, 2018. https://www.bbc.com/news/world-middle-east-42591334.

BBC News, "The Indian women abandoned because of mental illness," BBC News, October 16, 2018. https://www.bbc.com/news/world-asia-india-45861899.

Magdalena Cerdá, Magdalena Paczkowski, Sandro Galea, Kevin Nemethy, Claude Péan, Moïse Desvarieux, "Psychopathology in the Aftermath of the Haiti Earthquake: A Population-Based Study of Posttraumatic Stress Disorder and Major Depression," Depress Anxiety, May 2013. https://www.ncbi.nlm.nih.gov/pmc/articles/PMC3632660/.

Patrick Corrigan, "How Stigma Interferes With Mental Health Care," University of Chicago, 2004. http://www.academia.cat/files/425-8237-DOCUMENT/Howstigmainterfereswithmentalhealthcare.pdf.

Avi D'Souza, "Breaking: 3 Hospitals Bombed Today in Syria," ReliefWeb, May 5, 2019. https://reliefweb.int/report/syrian-arab-republic/breaking-3-hospitals-bombed-today-syria.

James Eusanio, "If you have symptoms of PTSD, don't wait to get help. Take it from an FS member who's been there." American Foreign Service Association. http://www.afsa.org/treating-ptsd-learning-firsthand-how-manage.

India Today Web Desk, "India is the most depressed country in the world," India Today, October 10, 2018. https://www.

indiatoday.in/education-today/gk-current-affairs/story/india-is-the-most-depressed-country-in-the-world-mental-health-day-2018-1360096-2018-10-10.

Laura Greenstein, "9 Ways To Fight Mental Health Stigma," National Alliance on Mental Illness, October 11, 2017. https://www.nami.org/blogs/nami-blog/october-2017/9-ways-to-fight-mental-health-stigma.

Erin Marcus, "PTSD Manifests Differently in Haitian Paitients, Says Researcher," HuffPost, December 6, 2017. https://www.huffpost.com/entry/ptsd-manifests-differentl_b_580825?guccounter=1&guce_referrer=aHR0cHM6Ly93d3cuZ29vZ2xlLmNvbS8&guce_referrer_sig=AQAAAKXxh3FsOd5s-2oCJqFK6xkvjrwf82ZJY2fQp-lAEBnL7R8V54rZlsV2ZuPHdHJ_kxgz1tZLC6iSEZBWWAfCeCuKQ7SIp4TKVFIDkvydxvJgbpFbe6V39BYtlqHQX0syPrr5a-3UFlUoCfRt9OqzBxixxFh_UKkWn240kV-GPWyk.

Mayo Clinic Staff, "Mental health: Overcoming the stigma of mental illness," Mayo Clinic, May 24, 2017. https://www.mayoclinic.org/diseases-conditions/mental-illness/in-depth/mental-health/art-20046477.

Marie Laurence Pierre-Louis, "Investigating Psychological Trauma Among the 2010 Haiti Earthquake Survivors Who Have Relocated to Boston, Massachusetts," Harvard Library Office for Scholarly Communication, April 2016. https://dash.harvard.edu/handle/1/33797323.

Syrian American Medical Society Foundation, "Impacts of attacks on healthcare in Syria," ReliefWeb, October 19, 2018. https://reliefweb.int/report/syrian-arab-republic/impacts-attacks-healthcare-syria.

Maria Thomas, "Charted: India's shocking attitudes towards mental illness," Quartz India, March 26, 2018. https://qz.com/india/1237314/fear-and-apathy-how-indians-look-at-those-suffering-mental-illnesses/.

What Has Impacted Women's Health Around the World?

In Guatemala and Peru Reproductive Rights Are Limited Because of a US Policy

Taylor Lewis

In the following viewpoint Taylor Lewis argues that women in Guatemala and Peru, as well as other parts of Latin America, will suffer from President Donald Trump's decision to reinstate the Mexico City Policy—also known as the Global Gag Rule. This rule cuts off U.S. funds to programs overseas that are involved in abortion-related activities, which includes counseling women on their reproductive choices. Not only has Trump reinstated the Global Gag Rule, but the administration has also placed restrictions that stop U.S. based doctors from providing not just family planning advice, but also HIV or tuberculosis treatment, child health care, nutrition programs, malaria treatments, and more. Taylor Lewis is research associate at the Council on Hemispheric Affairs.

As you read, consider the following questions:

1. Why is there a historic precedent for Republican presidents to institute the Global Gag Rule and for Democratic presidents to rescind it?

2. Why has there been an increase in abortions performed in Latin America and the Caribbean, according to the viewpoint?

3. What services and benefits other than abortion procedures are likely to be affected by enforcement of the Global Gag Rule?

With the inauguration of U.S. President Donald Trump on January 20, 2017, new challenges have emerged in the fight for women's reproductive rights around the world; specifically, Washington's decision to reinstate the Mexico City Policy on January 23. The Mexico City Policy, or the "global gag rule", as many NGOs refer to it, is an executive order that prohibits federal funding institutions such as the United States Agency for International Development (USAID), the Department of Defense, and the Peace Corps from funding non-governmental, non-profit organizations that "provide or promote" abortions or abortion related services around the world.[1]

Historically, the enforcement of this policy has been a partisan issue, dependent on presidential executive orders. Since the conception of the policy in 1984 under President Ronald Reagan, the Mexico City Policy has been rescinded by Democratic Presidents Bill Clinton in 1993 and Barack Obama in 2009, and re-enforced by former Republican President George W. Bush in 2001 and now President Donald Trump in 2017.[2] Despite this history, the most recent decision to reinstate the policy bears great weight on the operations of humanitarian efforts around the world, especially in Latin America and the Caribbean. According to *Forbes*, over the next four years, "international care organizations expect to lose $600 million in U.S. support," drastically limiting the scope of their operations.[3]

In a January report from *The Guardian*, shortly after Trump's announcement to reinstate the global gag rule, a spokeswoman for the International Planned Parenthood Federation (IPPF), which conducts family planning and maternal health services in a number of Latin American countries, including Guatemala, Ecuador, Nicaragua and Peru, announced that the group "will not abide by the Mexico City Policy" and "stands to lose up to $100 million USD" in federal benefits.[4] As a result, the organization predicts that it will be increasingly difficult to supply women with services such as safe and effective contraception, which are paid for largely by the $100 million dollars in U.S. foreign aid. As Amu Singh Sijapati, president of the Family Planning Association of Nepal, a member of IPPF, noted, without U.S. funding abroad, IPPF operations around the world "would not be able to run community clinics or mobile health days or train healthcare workers. The impact also means we would lose essential medical staff like nurses, doctors and health experts."[5]

Ms. Singh is not alone in her firm position that the Mexico City Policy is detrimental to the work of the IPPF. In a statement provided to the Council on Hemispheric Affairs (COHA) by Giselle Carino, Regional Director of International Planned Parenthood/ Western Hemisphere Region, Carino further explained why the organization refuses to abide by the global gag rule. "We refuse to sign a law that is anti-democratic, a law that undermines national sovereignty, limits the right to free speech and the ability of our providers to provide the best care to all. Finally, we refuse to sign a law that plays with women's lives and flies in the face of public health research that shows that banning the procedure leads to more death and injury for women, particularly the poorest women. We will continue to stand with women worldwide in condemning this unfair and dangerous policy."[6]

The IPPF is not the only NGO that stands to suffer at the hand of the global gag rule. Population Services International (PSI), an international organization based in Washington, D.C. and operating in a number of Latin American countries, including Honduras, Guatemala and El Salvador, which fights for women's reproductive rights not only by providing post-abortion care, but by providing contraceptives, sexual education and STI prevention services, has historically depended on grants from the federal government to fund its operations. In 2014, two of PSI's donors were USAID and the United States Department of Defense. Together, these federal funds suppliers provided the organization a combined total of more than $120,000 in grant money, but now, PSI may be forced to make a difficult decision about the future of its operations if it wishes to receive the same level of funding.[7]

From past implementations of the Mexico City Policy, a 2011 quantitative analysis by Stanford University researchers Eran Bendavid, Patrick Avila and Grant Miller demonstrated that the restrictions have historically led to the inverse effects of the policy's theoretical goal of limiting abortions in developing countries. Abortion rates were found to be higher in countries with high exposure to the Mexico City Policy (countries that received humanitarian aid from non-governmental organizations) compared to those with low exposure. Focusing their analysis on 20 sub-Saharan African countries, the researchers found that between 1994 and 2001, while the Mexico City Policy was not in effect, the induced abortion rate was about 10 per 10, 000 women, while between 2001 and 2008, with George W. Bush's reinstatement of the policy, the rate jumped to 14.5 per 10 000 women.[8] Additionally, the use of modern contraceptive techniques declined over the same period of time in high exposure countries compared to low exposure countries.[9] The reason for this trend is likely that the NGOs that were barred from federal funding had fewer resources at hand to support maternal and family planning services. Without resources to provide important contraceptives, which reduce unintended pregnancies and ultimately limit the need for abortions, NGOs are unable to assist women in the developing world as they have been in the past, leading to an increase in abortion, both legal and illegal. Additionally, in the impoverished and indigenous regions of Latin America, where contraception and reproductive services are scarce, without NGO's offering safe and sufficient support, women are put at a dangerous disadvantage.

The rescinding of the Mexico City Policy does not suddenly stop direct United States funding for abortion internationally, as that has already been the case for decades. In fact, direct government funding for abortion has been restricted since the 1970s, when the Helms Amendment of 1973 prohibited the use of United States aid in paying for the abortion as a method of family planning. Furthermore, in 1981, the Biden Amendment prevented federal funding for biomedical research related to methods of or the performance of abortions overseas, which makes this kind of restriction a bipartisan issue.[10] In the face of the Mexico City Policy, then, these provisions remind us that the policy itself is not only a reflection of a U.S. policy to push a pro-life global agenda, but is instead an overreaching step by the executive branch that has curbed the efforts of non-governmental agencies and harmed the health of women in the most disparate regions around the world.

Looking Ahead: the Mexico City Policy's Impact on Latin America

To understand the implications of Trump's Mexico City Policy in the Latin American context, it is important to first recognize the increasingly high demand for abortion-related health services in the region and the key role that international NGOs have historically played in providing them. According to a 2016 analysis from the Guttmacher institute, a research and policy organization committed to advancing global sexual and reproductive health, in Latin America and the Caribbean, the number of abortions performed between 2010 and 2014 was 6.5 million, while two decades earlier, between 1990 and 1994, the abortion rate was only 4.4 million.[11] Given this increase, which likely corresponded with overall population growth, in 2015, researchers Susheela Singh and Isaac Maddow-Zimmer found that roughly 760,000 women in Latin America and the Caribbean are treated annually for complications as a result of to unsafe abortions.[12] With such great demand for abortion related health services and stringent regional policies in place that limit sufficient access to such services, it is necessary that the proper providers are in place and are prepared to serve those in need. With the reinstatement of the Mexico City Policy, however, these services will only become harder to render, especially in the poorer, indigenous communities of places such as Guatemala and Peru.

Guatemala

In Guatemala, abortion is legal, but only to save the life of the woman. This law is significant because its window for legal abortions allows organizations such as the IPPF, PSI and other NGOs to offer family planning services with minimal restriction from the government. With this freedom, NGOs have come to fill a great void in health care service for the women of the region. In Guatemala, it is estimated that less than one third of women are taught about basic sexual and reproductive health, while only 25 percent receive information about contraception.[13]

In 2015, a satellite of IPPF, the Association for Family Well Being of Guatemala (APROFAM) was the largest NGO providing sexual and reproductive health care in Guatemala, operating 27 clinics and 5 mobile health units. In the same year, the organization provided 1.6 million services for Guatemalan women, including gynecological care, contraceptives and STI prevention and testing.[14] With aid from USAID, which is now on the verge of ceasing such funds, APROFAM has been able to push for an increase in national awareness for basic reproductive health and access to contraception though its peer education program, which "disseminates information and encourages young people to seek its subsidized care."[15] Without the funding that APROFAM needs to continue the same level of service, the women of the region will be at a great loss.

Peru

In Peru, like Guatemala, abortion is only legal in cases in which the mother's life is in danger, but this still allows for the presence of NGOs and health providers that provide family planning and post abortion care. In a country where more than 50 percent of the rural population lives below the poverty line (over 3 million people) and relatively conservative reproduction laws keep women from being able to access basic reproductive health coverage (in 2015, the Peruvian Congress voted against a bill that would legalize abortions in the case of rape), there is great demand, even if not publicized, for maternal health care, sexual education and abortion related care.[16, 17]

Given this immense demand, the Peruvian Institute of Responsible Parenting (INPPARES), the IPPF's satellite organization in Peru, has been a reliable care provider. In 2015, the organization ran 17 clinics nationwide and had 7 mobile health units, providing 400,000 individual services over the course of the year.[18]

In Peru, direct health care is not the only service at risk of being lost as a result of the United States' defunding of organizations such as IPPF. In fact, some of the most impactful measures taken by sexual and reproductive rights-centered NGOs overseas are their partnerships with local grassroots organizations that seek to promote basic human rights. In Lima, Peru, the IPPF has done just that with Promsex, a women's and reproductive rights group that has been fighting to repeal the country's stringent reproductive laws since the organization's conception in 2005. In 2015, Planned Parenthood and IPPF gave $648,000 USD to Promsex to fund its advocacy and research efforts, aiding in the organization's mission to "promote and defend equality in diversity and the full exercise of sexual and reproductive rights."[19, 20]

According to the Promsex website, data and advocacy provided by the organization has played an important role in the drafting of Congressional bills in Peru since 2005, covering a range of issues, including "hate crimes, decriminalizing consensual sex in people under 18 years of age, civil unions between people of the same sex, the decriminalization of abortion by causal rape, compliance of therapeutic abortion and access for adolescents to sexual and reproductive health."[21] While not all bills have passed, the work that Promsex has accomplished to advance the basic rights of Peruvian citizens has been a beacon of hope for those who wish to see a more progressive and equitable society.

Ultimately, the situation in Guatemala and Peru demonstrates that the effects of the United States' reinstatement of the Mexico City Policy are likely to trickle down to affect the most vulnerable citizens of Latin America. Much like the less fortunate citizens of Guatemala who have come to rely on the services of health care providing organizations like APROFAM for maternal and post abortion care, Peruvian women now find themselves in a position of uncertainty, unaware of how much help they may be able to expect from organizations like INPPARES and Promsex in the future.

Global Responses to the Mexico City Policy

In the wake of the decision to reinstate the global gag rule, other countries have stepped up to address the cessation of funds to humanitarian efforts by the United States. Most notably, the Dutch government has led a charge for global fundraising, in hopes of offsetting the deficit that will undeniably impact the work of NGOs around the world. Lilianne Ploumen, the Minister for Foreign Trade and Development Cooperation for the Netherlands, has launched the new "She Decides—Global Fundraising Initiative" program, which seeks to garner worldwide support for the organizations that will no longer benefit from the estimated $600 million USD aid from the U.S. government.[22]

The Dutch government has pledged 10 million euros ($10.7 million USD) to the cause, and continues working to encourage other countries to make pledges of their own. In an interview with the Guardian, Minister Ploumen said that: "As well as contacting a number of European countries that we work with on these issues, we're also in touch with countries in South America and Africa."[23] On the program's website, shedecides.eu, users are invited to make donations as well.

Minister Ploumen's efforts offer great encouragement to non-profit organizations and indigenous women alike, but they also set an important precedent that governments must not turn their backs on the lives of those in need. As Ploumen urged, "we cannot let women and girls down. They should have the right to decide if they want to have children, when they want to have children, and with who they want to have children."[24]

However honorable Pluomen's stance may be, in light of the United States' seemingly limited perspective on humanitarian efforts around the world, her message requires more action now than ever if progress for women's rights around the world is to be attained.

Notes

1. "The Mexico City Policy: An Explainer." Kaiser Family Foundation – Health Policy Research, Analysis, Polling, Facts, Data and Journalism. 23, 2017 Jan. http://kff.org/global-health-policy/fact-sheet/mexico-city-policy-explainer/.
2. "The Mexico City Policy: An Explainer." Kaiser Family Foundation – Health Policy Research, Analysis, Polling, Facts, Data and Journalism. 23, 2017 Jan. http://kff.org/global-health-policy/fact-sheet/mexico-city-policy-explainer/.
3. Burns, Janet. "Dutch Give $10.7M To Fund Women's Global Health After Trump Imperils It." Forbes. January 30, 2017. http://www.forbes.com/sites/janetwburns/2017/01/30/dutch-give-10-7m-to-fund-womens-global-health-after-trump-imperils-it/#72a9a0ccad6c.

4. Redden, Molly. "'Global gag rule' reinstated by Trump, curbing NGO abortion services abroad." The Guardian. January 23, 2017. https://www.theguardian.com/world/2017/jan/23/trump-abortion-gag-rule-international-ngo-funding.

5. Redden, Molly. "'Global gag rule' reinstated by Trump, curbing NGO abortion services abroad." The Guardian. January 23, 2017. https://www.theguardian.com/world/2017/jan/23/trump-abortion-gag-rule-international-ngo-funding.

6. Carino, Giselle. Statement on Global Gag Rule. February 28, 2017.

7. "USAID PVO Registry." USAID PVO Registry. http://pvo.usaid.gov/usaid/pvo.asp?i=184&INCVOLAG=YES&INCSUM=YES&VolagText=.

8. "United States Aid Policy and Induced Abortion in Sub-Saharan Africa." WHO. http://www.who.int/bulletin/volumes/89/12/11-091660/en/.

9. Bendavid, Eran , Patrick Avila, and Grant Miller. "United States Aid Policy and Induced Abortion in Sub-Saharan Africa." WHO. June 07, 2011. http://www.who.int/bulletin/volumes/89/12/11-091660/en/.

10. 23, 2017 Jan. "The Mexico City Policy: An Explainer." Kaiser Family Foundation – Health Policy Research, Analysis, Polling, Facts, Data and Journalism. http://kff.org/global-health-policy/fact-sheet/mexico-city-policy-explainer/.

11. "Abortion in Latin America and the Caribbean." Guttmacher Institute. August 03, 2016. https://www.guttmacher.org/fact-sheet/facts-abortion-latin-america-and-caribbean#2.

12. Singh, S., and I. Maddow-Zimet. "Facility-based treatment for medical complications resulting from unsafe pregnancy termination in the developing world, 2012: a review of evidence from 26 countries." BJOG: An International Journal of Obstetrics & Gynaecology123, no. 9 (2015): 1489-498. doi:10.1111/1471-0528.13552.

13. "APROFAM." Ippfwhr.org. https://www.ippfwhr.org/en/country/guatemala.

14. "APROFAM." Ippfwhr.org. https://www.ippfwhr.org/en/country/guatemala.

15. "APROFAM." Ippfwhr.org. https://www.ippfwhr.org/en/country/guatemala.

16. "Rural Poverty in Peru ." Https://www.ruralpovertyportal.org/country/home/tags/peru. 2014.

17. Moloney, Anastasia. "Peru lawmakers reject bill to allow pregnant rape victims an abortion." Reuters. May 27, 2015. http://www.reuters.com/article/us-peru-abortion-rights-idUSKBN0OC2CI20150527.

18. "INPPARES ." Ippfwhr.org. https://www.ippfwhr.org/en/country/peru.

19. Prensa, Actuall / Aci, Pablo González De Castejón, Beatriz De La Rosa, and Ana Fuentes. "Promsex en Perú recibió más de medio millón de euros de Planned Parenthood en 2015." Actuall. March 28, 2016. http://www.actuall.com/vida/promsex-en-peru-recibio-mas-de-medio-millon-de-dolares-de-planned-parenthood-en-2015/.

20. "Visión y Misión." Promsex. http://www.promsex.org/index.php/acerca-de-promsex/mision-y-vision.

21. "Memoria Institucional 2010 – 2013." Promsex. http://www.promsex.org/index.php/logros.

22. "She Decides, You Can Help!" She Decides, You Can Help! https://www.shedecides.eu/.

23. "Dutch respond to Trump's 'gag rule' with international safe abortion fund." Women's Rights and Gender Equality. January 25, 2017. https://www.theguardian.com/global-development/2017/jan/25/netherlands-trump-gag-rule-international-safe-abortion-fund.

24. "Minister Ploumen launches 'SHE DECIDES'" Ministerie van Algemene Zaken. January 28, 2017. https://www.government.nl/latest/news/2017/01/28/minister-ploumen-launches-she-decides.

In the United States Sexism Is Alive and Well in the Healthcare Industry

Julia Haskins

In the following viewpoint, Julia Haskins argues that, on the surface, it may seem that there is a growing equality for women in the healthcare field, but in actuality, women working in healthcare still encounter the stereotypical glass ceiling and face sexism and discrimination that keeps them out of positions of influence around the world. In 2012, it was reported by the Association of American Medical Colleges (AAMC) that just 15 percent of department chairs are women and only 16 percent are deans. Additionally, it was reported that only 18 percent of women were hospital CEOs. These statistics mean that women are not in positions to enact meaningful policy changes that would help improve healthcare for women overall. Julia Haskins is a staff writer for the Association of American Medical Colleges.

As you read, consider the following questions:

1. According to the viewpoint, how does the handoff of independent pharmacies impact the ability for women to advance in the medical field?
2. Why are women and minorities in surgical training programs less likely to receive board certification?
3. What are some of the hardship that women face in healthcare, especially for those who are pursuing their careers?

On the surface, the outlook is promising for women in healthcare.

Women and men are enrolling in medical school at similar rates and women hold a wide range of positions in the healthcare industry.

They're inspiring a new generation of women in a field once thought to be the domain of men.

However, women are still being held back from attaining positions of influence in the medical world.

They also regularly contend with sexism and discrimination before hitting the proverbial glass ceiling.

What healthcare consumers may not realize is that unfair treatment of women has repercussions. Medical communities lose out on crucial perspectives.

Unequal Representation

Women make up about one-third of the physicians in the United States, most in areas such as family medicine, obstetrics and gynecology, and pediatrics.

How about chief executives, medical school deans, and department chairs?

According to data from the Association of American Medical Colleges (AAMC), just 15 percent of department chairs are women and only 16 percent are deans. By 2012, just 18 percent of women were hospital CEOs.

"When you're talking about the positions of authority in healthcare, people who can really make systemic changes to address healthcare needs … women are not in these positions to enact policy changes," said Diana Lautenberger, director of Women in Medicine and Science for the AAMC.

Pharmacology is one area of healthcare in which women are thriving, but they are still grappling with policies and norms rooted in sexism.

On the whole, pharmacology is a rewarding field for women, allowing for flexibility and yielding relatively high earnings. However, few women own pharmacies, which may restrict their opportunities and authority.

Part of the problem lies in the handoff of independent pharmacies, according to Eden Sulzer, director of Women in Pharmacy at Cardinal Health.

Male pharmacy owners who don't have successors often get their businesses snapped up by chain pharmacies because women with all of the right qualifications may still not feel comfortable taking the leap into business ownership.

"Women are essentially talking themselves out of business ownership because of fear. Fear of risk, fear of not being able to have a personal life and a family life, so they're going into other fields," Sulzer said.

In hospitals and other healthcare settings, the imbalance in power is also visible.

"When you look at these subspecialties that really have authority … that's where we see the underrepresentation," Lautenberger said.

Take surgeons, for example. Research shows that women and minorities in general surgical training programs are less likely than males to attain board certification. The reasons why are not fully understood, but surgery can be an unwelcoming environment for women.

Gender-Based Job Restrictions Around the World

A recent World Bank survey of 173 countries found that no fewer than 155 still had at least one law impeding women's economic opportunities. Women face gender-based job restrictions in 100 countries, often confining them to low-paying activities, more often than not in the informal sector. In 18 countries the law gives husbands the right to prohibit their wives from working outside the home.

These legal differences have long-lasting economic and social consequences. Gender based job restrictions tend to be associated with wider wage gaps and lower employment rates for women. And where girls' future earning potential is limited, families may choose to send their brothers to school instead.

Laws matter. With effective implementation and enforcement, good laws can nudge forward positive changes in social and cultural mores. Legislating parental leave—for fathers as opposed to only for new mothers—has been shown to promote a more equitable division of childrearing responsibilities. Legal changes to human resources procedures, and reinforcing equal pay for comparable work, could help offset cultural biases that work against women who ask for a raise. Research shows that more equal laws boost women's participation in the workforce.

Dr. Yvette Canaba, a podiatric surgeon and physician at St. John's Episcopal Hospital in New York, is familiar with the dilemma.

"It's always had that belief that females are unable to withstand the pressures that one experiences in the operating room," Canaba said. "You have a patient's life at stake and, depending on the surgery, there's the belief that women are the weaker sex and are unable to withstand the emotional and physical stressors that accompany that kind of a setting."

Last year's #ILookLikeASurgeon campaign sought to highlight women surgeons, shaking up notions of who a surgeon can be. Still, some outdated views of women in surgery persist.

"We go through the same schooling, the same training as our male counterparts. We took the same examinations as our male

And it's not just about the workplace. Women in several countries face extra documentation hurdles when trying to get a national identity card. Beyond making it tougher to access public services or contracts with others, no proof of ID means no chance of getting a bank loan to start or expand a business. Inheritance and marital property laws affect women's access to financial institutions – access to property tends to make for greater equality within the household.

The economic cost of gender inequality is staggering. The McKinsey Global Institute recently estimated that if women participated in the economy identically to men, with equal wages and labour force participation, it would add up to $28tn to global GDP by 2025: a 26% increase over business as usual, equivalent to adding a new United States and China to the world economy.

A more modest scenario, under which countries match the gender parity progress of their best-performing regional neighbour, would add $12tn to the global economy – about the collective economic weight of Japan, Germany, and the UK.

The implications are no less revolutionary for individual households. Literate mothers have healthier children. When women earn an income, they spend a higher proportion of it than men do on their children's health, education and nutrition.

"In 155 countries women still face legal discrimination. The consequences are huge," by Arancha González, Guardian News and Media Limited, December 3, 2015.

counterparts. There's no reason to believe that we can't deliver equal quality care as our male counterparts," Canaba said.

Hardships Facing Women in Healthcare

As a medical student at the University of Illinois at Chicago, Karishma Bhatt is not naive to the challenges she faces as she pursues a career as a surgeon.

Bhatt wanted to get a better sense of what sexism looks like in medicine, so she asked users on Reddit's medical schools subreddit about their experiences.

Respondents told her about how female physicians are regularly mistaken for other roles, which Bhatt called "relatively innocuous" in an article for in-Training.

But some stories eclipsed the condescending, run-of-the-mill comments. Reddit users discussed how being pregnant can threaten career prospects and the ways sexual harassment permeates healthcare.

Bhatt wasn't completely surprised by what she learned.

"Sexism is really pervasive in a really stressful field such as medicine," making it "easy to fall back on stereotypes," Bhatt said.

An emergency room physician once told Bhatt about a related phenomenon. Throughout the course of their residencies, some emergency room doctors may succumb to the pressures of the job, becoming more racist and sexist by the end of the year. In such a demanding environment, Bhatt said, confirmation bias can reinforce negative stereotypes.

And women may already be forced to tread lightly for fear of giving any credence to unfair depictions.

"More often than not an assertive female is looked at is someone who's bitchy or moody or not friendly. It still happens and I'm already a senior in my program," Cabana said.

"It's very interesting," she noted, "how even in this day and age when you're an assertive female it's not something that's applauded. It's something that's automatically attributed to a woman's emotional state."

Trickle-Down Effect

For the first two years in her residency, Canaba was the only woman.

"It was very easy for the male counterparts in my group to kind of set me aside when it came to making decisions for the plan of care for patients," she said.

Canaba's experience is just one sliver of a widespread matter. When women are left out of the conversation, so are their insights and expertise.

"In the end it's the patient that loses," Canaba said. "Our patient population as a whole definitely benefits from a more diverse group of physicians that is in charge of their care."

Female patients may also benefit from providers with a more personal stake in their health. They may also feel more comfortable discussing their medical issues.

"We need people in these rooms treating people that look like them and someone they can identify with," Lautenberg said.

That's also true of interactions that take place outside of the hospital.

"The reason why I feel so passionately about this beyond empowering women … is patient care is going to be delivered outside the hospital," Sulzer said. "Pharmacists really are that first line of healthcare in many communities."

To Sulzer, it makes sense to have women at the forefront.

"Women make [most of the] healthcare purchasing decisions, so I say who better to serve them than female pharmacists in their communities," she said.

The loss of women's perspectives is notable in academic medicine as well. One study found that female biomedical researchers receive significantly less financial support early in their careers compared with their male counterparts.

Lautenberger also points to the National Institutes of Health (NIH) policy on the Consideration of Sex as a Biological Variable, which was spurred by the high volume of research that uses only male patients, stem cells, and even mice in clinical and biomedical trials.

"That's a perfect example of what we lose as a society when we leave out half of the population," Lautenberger said.

What Can Be Done?

The issues affecting healthcare have plagued numerous other industries and experts say reform is needed at all levels of healthcare to turn the tide.

From an administrative standpoint, hospitals and healthcare systems need to step up their standards of parity, with fair pay being one part of the equation.

A recent study from Glassdoor found that the pay gap between men and women is especially pronounced in healthcare.

Bhatt proposes a cultural shift in hospitals, emphasizing the need for fair hiring standards and women-friendly policies such as maternity leave. That also includes creating a safe work environment in which even the most well respected, tenured physicians are subject to scrutiny for complaints of sexual harassment.

"It doesn't matter that you have tenure, you're harassing the future of medicine," Bhatt said.

Helping patients and healthcare consumers become more aware of the ways in which they contribute to sexist behavior is another hurdle for equity.

"Very often we find the patients have their own biases toward these women [providers]," Lautenberg said.

According to Bhatt, the stressful environment of a hospital may serve as the catalyst for sexist behavior.

"When we see patients it's everyday for us, for a patient it might be the worst day of their life," she said.

Patients may lash out with sexist comments without meaning to, making an already tense situation more difficult.

Lautenberger suggests that patients examine their unconscious biases not only to show more respect toward female providers but also to open themselves up to the best possible care, which may just happen to be administered by a woman.

"As a patient and as a consumer, becoming more aware of your biases and what you are preferential to may allow you to make more informed decisions in terms of providers," Lautenberg said.

To push back against sexism in healthcare, women are turning to one another for support through mentoring and educational programs led by other women in the field.

AAMC's Women in Medicine, Cardinal Health's Women in Pharmacy, and SEIU Healthcare's Women in Medicine group, all offer various programs and tools to help women navigate their careers in healthcare.

Topics like salary negotiation, leadership, and promotion reflect the challenges that women in medicine face every day on the job.

"The additional mentoring and education you need to … make it as a woman in science is really quite substantial," Lautenberg said.

As women in healthcare embark on their careers, they need as much support as they can get.

Canaba wants women in medicine to know that "they're not alone."

"There's always going to be someone out there who has not been afraid to speak out and move forward despite these things," she said. "Seek them out for mentorship and support because they're out there."

Cardiovascular Disease Kills 40 Percent of Women

Texas Heart Institute

In the following viewpoint, the Texas Heart Institute details how heart disease is responsible for more than 40 percent of all deaths in American women. With the life expectancy for women in the United States at 79 years, one in four women older than 65 is likely to have some form of heart disease. This likelihood is exacerbated by hormone replacement therapies (HRT) that are often prescribed for symptoms of menopause, including bone-based diseases like osteoporosis. Smoking is a major risk factor for heart disease, and while the overall number of adult smokers has decreased over the last 20 years, there is an uptick in the number girls who smoke. Those girls who smoke and use birth control are even more likely to have a heart attack or stroke. The Texas Heart Institute is dedicated to cardiovascular discovery and innovation.

As you read, consider the following questions:

1. Why were women historically undertreated for heart disease?
2. Per the viewpoint, what are the differences in symptoms of a heart attack for men and women?
3. What are some of the factors that lead to an increased risk for heart disease in women specifically?

Heart disease is no longer considered a disease that affects just men. In the past, women usually received less aggressive treatment for heart disease and were not referred for diagnostic tests as often. As a result, when many women were finally diagnosed with heart disease, they usually had more advanced disease and their prognosis was poorer. We now know that cardiovascular diseases affect more women than men and are responsible for more than 40% of all deaths in American women.

Women and Heart Attacks

Heart attack symptoms in women may be different from those experienced by men. Many women who have a heart attack do not know it. Women tend to feel a burning sensation in their upper abdomen and may experience lightheadedness, an upset stomach, and sweating. Because they may not feel the typical pain in the left half of their chest, many women may ignore symptoms that indicate they are having a heart attack.

Heart attacks are generally more severe in women than in men. In the first year after a heart attack, women are more than 50% more likely to die than men are. In the first 6 years after a heart attack, women are almost twice as likely to have a second heart attack.

Estrogen and Heart Disease

Studies have shown that after menopause, women experience an increased risk of heart disease. Researchers have connected this pattern to decreasing levels of the female hormone estrogen during menopause—a process that begins around age 50. Estrogen is associated with higher levels of high-density lipoprotein (HDL or "good cholesterol") and lower levels of low-density lipoprotein (LDL or "bad cholesterol"). Withdrawal of the natural estrogen that occurs in menopause leads to lower "good cholesterol" and higher "bad cholesterol" thus increasing the risk of heart disease. Because the life expectancy for women in the United States is 79 years, women can expect to live a large part of their lives with an increased risk of heart disease. In fact, 1 out of 4 women older than 65 has some form of identified heart disease.

Researchers have looked at how hormone replacement therapy (HRT) may affect women who already have heart disease and those who don't. After several years of study and numerous clinical trials with differing results, the AHA still does not advise women to take HRT to reduce the risk of coronary heart disease or stroke. Women should weigh the risks of HRT and discuss them with their doctor. For the symptoms of menopause, including bone loss, effective non-hormonal treatments are available.

Modifiable Risk Factors for Women

Women need to be aware of the risk factors for cardiovascular disease and the importance of making lifestyle changes that may reduce those risks. Factors such as race, increasing age, and a family history of heart disease cannot be changed. Other risk factors, however, can be changed or eliminated by making informed decisions about cardiovascular health.

Smoking is a major risk factor for cardiovascular disease. Although the overall number of adult smokers has decreased in this country during the last 20 years, the number of teenaged girls who smoke has increased. Cigarette smoking combined with the use of birth control pills greatly increases the risk of heart attack or stroke. The good news is that no matter how long or how much someone has smoked, smokers can immediately reduce their risk of heart attack by quitting. After 1 year of not smoking, the excess risk of heart disease created by smoking is reduced 80%; after 7 years of not smoking, all the risk from smoking is gone. It is never too late to stop smoking.

High blood pressure, or hypertension is a silent disease. If left untreated, it makes the heart work harder, speeds up hardening of the arteries (atherosclerosis), and increases the risk of heart attack, stroke, and kidney failure. Women who have a history of high blood pressure, black women with high blood pressure, and overweight women with high blood pressure are also at greater risk. Although high blood pressure cannot be cured, it can be controlled with diet, exercise, and, if necessary, medicines. High blood pressure is a lifelong risk and requires effective long-term management, including regular blood pressure checks and the appropriate medicines.

Pregnancy may trigger high blood pressure, especially during the third trimester, but high blood pressure caused by pregnancy usually goes away after childbirth. This is called pregnancy-induced hypertension. Another form of high blood pressure that can occur during pregnancy is called preeclampsia, and it is usually accompanied by swelling and increased protein in the urine. Women with a history of preeclampsia face double the risk of stroke, heart disease and dangerous clotting in their veins during the 5 to 15 years after pregnancy.

Cholesterol levels are also related to a person's risk of heart disease. Doctors look at how your levels of LDL, HDL, and fats called triglycerides relate to each other and to your total cholesterol level. Before menopause, women in general have higher cholesterol levels than men because estrogen increases HDL levels in the blood. A study reported in the American Journal of Cardiology found that HDL levels were one of the most important predictor of cardiovascular health. That is, the higher a woman's HDL level, the less likely she is to have a cardiovascular event such as heart attack or stroke. But after menopause, HDL levels tend to drop, increasing the risk of heart disease. HDL and LDL cholesterol levels can be improved by diet, exercise, and, in serious cases, statins or other cholesterol-lowering medicines.

Obesity is a strong predictor for heart disease, especially among women. A person is considered obese if body weight exceeds the "desirable" weight for height and gender by 20 percent or more. Where fat settles on the body is also an important predictor. Women who have a lot of fat around the waist are at greater risk than those who have fat around the hips. In the United States, about one third of women are classified as obese. A plan of diet

Who Has a Higher Risk of Heart Attack?

Certain diseases that only affect women increase the risk of coronary artery disease, the leading cause of heart attack. These include endometriosis, polycystic ovary disease, diabetes and high blood pressure that develop during pregnancy. Endometriosis has been found to raise the risk of developing CAD by 400 percent in women under age 40.

Men are at risk for heart attack much earlier in life than women. Estrogen offers women some protection from heart disease until after menopause, when estrogen levels drop. This is why the average age of for a heart attack is 70 in women, but 66 in men.

Chest pain is the most common symptom of heart attack in men. Some women also experience chest pain, but they are more likely to have different symptoms. Unlike the dramatic, chest-clutching pain seen in the movies, women often experience subtler symptoms for three or four weeks before a heart attack. Red flags include:

- New or dramatic fatigue. For example, a simple activity like making the bed makes you feel unusually tired. You aren't exerting yourself, but you feel deeply fatigued or have a "heavy" chest. You may feel very tired, but can't sleep well. Or you are suddenly worn out after your normal exercise routine.

- Shortness of breath or sweating. Watch for this especially when either symptom occurs without exertion and when either symptom is accompanied by a symptom such a chest pain or fatigue. Look for either symptom worsening over time after exertion. Other signs are shortness of breath that worsens when lying down and is relieved when you sit up and a cold, clammy feeling that occurs without cause.

- Pain in the neck, back or jaw. This is especially of note when there is no specific muscle or joint that aches or when the discomfort worsens when you are exerting yourself and stops when you stop. This pain can be in either arm, whereas it's usually the left arm in men. Also, watch for pain that starts in the chest and spreads to the back, pain that occurs suddenly and may wake you up at night and pain in the lower left side of the jaw.

"Women or Men—Who Has a Higher Risk of Heart Attack?",
by Leslie Cho, Cleveland Clinic, February 17, 2017.

and exercise approved by your doctor is the best way to safely lose weight.

Diabetes is more common in overweight, less active women and poses a greater risk because it cancels the protective effects of estrogen in premenopausal women. Results of one study showed that women with diabetes have a higher risk of death from cardiovascular disease than men with diabetes have. The increased risk may also be explained by the fact that most diabetic patients tend to be overweight and physically inactive, have high cholesterol levels, and are more likely to have high blood pressure. Proper management of diabetes is important for cardiovascular health.

Other diseases and conditions, such as lupus and rheumatoid arthritis, can also increase a woman's risk of heart disease. According to new guidelines released by the AHA, illnesses linked to a higher risk of cardiovascular disease should now be incorporated into a woman's overall risk factor evaluation.

Physical inactivity is a significant risk factor for heart disease, yet millions of Americans still don't exercise at all. Many studies have shown that exercise reduces the risk of heart attack and stroke, increases HDL cholesterol levels, regulates glucose, lowers blood pressure, and increases the flexibility of arteries. Exercise has also been shown to reduce mental stress as well. You can benefit from exercising even it is only for 30 minutes a day, at least three times a week, but more will reap better benefits.

Oral contraceptives (birth control pills) may pose an increased cardiovascular risk for women, especially those with other risk factors such as smoking. Researchers believe that birth control pills raise blood pressure and blood sugar levels in some women, as well as increase the risk of blood clots. The risks associated with birth control pills increase as women get older. Women should tell their doctors about any other cardiovascular risk factors they have before they begin taking birth control pills.

Excessive alcohol intake can contribute to obesity, raise triglyceride and blood pressure levels, cause heart failure, and lead to stroke. Although studies have shown that the risk of heart disease in people who drink moderate amounts of alcohol is lower than in nondrinkers, this does not mean that nondrinkers should start drinking alcohol or that those who do drink should increase the amount they drink. For women, a moderate amount of alcohol is an average of one drink per day.

Stress is considered a contributing risk factor for both sexes, especially as it leads to other risk factors such as smoking and overeating.

Depression can affect how women deal with their health issues or follow their doctor's advice. According to American Heart Association guidelines, depression screening should now be part of an overall evaluation of women for cardiovascular risk.

Many risk factors that contribute to heart disease can be controlled. Quitting smoking, losing weight, exercising, lowering cholesterol and blood pressure, controlling diabetes, and reducing stress are within every woman's grasp.

In South Africa High Maternal Mortality Rates Are Preventable

Anja Smith

In the following viewpoint, Anja Smith details the high rate of maternal mortality in South Africa. In the country, for every 100,000 live births in 2015, there were 138 deaths due to pregnancy and childbirth complications. In comparison, in Sweden fewer than 5 women die for every 100,000 live births, while in Brazil the estimate is 44 deaths for every 100,000 live births. Many women in South Africa do not visit antenatal (prenatal) clinics until their fifth month of pregnancy, which is commonly considered very late. Part of the issues are policy-related, as pregnancy tests are not offered as commonly in South Africa as condoms, so it takes a longer time for many women, especially those who live in poverty, to discover that they are pregnant. Anja Smith is postdoctoral fellow at the Research on Socio-Economic Policy unit in the Economics Department of Stellenbosch University.

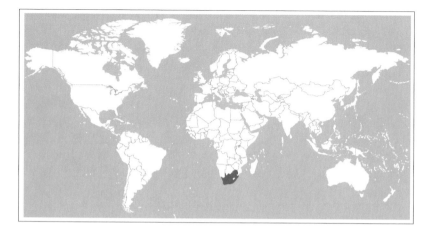

As you read, consider the following questions:

1. If women in South Africa are most likely to give birth in a hospital, why is the maternal mortality rate so high?

2. What impacts to cultural beliefs have on a woman's likelihood to receive antenatal care? How can those beliefs be overcome so women get the care they need?

3. How does education level impact a woman's likelihood to receive antenatal care?

S outh Africa has extremely high maternal mortality levels. This is true when compared with developed countries as well as other developing countries.

According to the World Health Organisation, for every 100,000 live births in the country in 2015, 138 women died due to pregnancy and childbirth complications. In Sweden, fewer than five women die for every 100,000 live births. In Brazil, the estimate is 44 women for every 100,000 live births.

Many of these deaths are preventable. And in South Africa—unlike many other developing countries—women mostly give birth in health-care facilities and visit antenatal clinics before they give birth. So why are the maternal mortality rates so high?

Earlier research has shown many women attend antenatal care for the first time too late in their pregnancies. This is due to:

- overburdened clinics, resulting in many being turned away without help;

- bad treatment by health-care workers, resulting in women devaluing the service;

- their fear of testing HIV positive and the associated stigma; and

- their cultural beliefs—that they may be bewitched by jealous neighbours or friends.

But our research shows that many women visit antenatal care clinics late because they discover they are pregnant late into their pregnancies.

Why Women Avoid Antenatal Clinics

Antenatal care services are mostly provided at community clinics that also provide a variety of general and primary health-care services to the community. These include care for HIV, TB and lifestyle diseases. These clinics tend to be busy and staff are often overburdened and overworked. All patients, including pregnant women, often have to wait for a long time before being seen by a nurse or doctor.

We interviewed women at public health-care facilities, including hospitals and birth facilities, in an urban area in the Western Cape province shortly after they had given birth.

More than a quarter of the women interviewed went to the clinic late into their pregnancies. Women who went to the clinic for the first time when they were five months pregnant were classified as attending a clinic late. But if attending an antenatal clinic at or after three months of pregnancy was considered late—attending after the first trimester is usually considered late—almost four in five women said they went late.

More than half of the women who said they sought antenatal care late did not go to the clinic early enough because they realised quite late that they were pregnant. Some said they purposefully postponed the visit. And more than two-thirds of the women who went late said nothing about the clinic would have made them go earlier.

The study showed that women who went late were more likely than those who went early to not have completed high school. Women who went late were also more likely to be poor. And compared with those women who attended clinics early into their pregnancies, these women were also more likely to say they consumed alcohol while they were pregnant.

We did not find evidence to show that late attendance was related to travel costs to access antenatal care at free public clinics.

But the relationship between poverty, education and general vulnerable circumstances is complex. While our research shows that women who attend antenatal care clinics later are likely to be poorer and have less education than women who attend early, we cannot say this is necessarily true for all poor or less-educated women. But poverty and lower education levels may make it more difficult for people to make the best choices about when to seek health care.

Why Early Antenatal Visits Are Important

The World Health Organisation recommends at least four visits to an antenatal clinic during pregnancy. Although South African women almost make this target, their late attendance has an impact on the ability of the health-care system to influence their health and that of their babies.

Attending an antenatal clinic early in pregnancy is important for two reasons.

First, if pregnant women attend the clinics in the first three months of their pregnancy, HIV can be detected early and they can begin treatment. This makes it less likely that their babies will contract HIV. It also helps to support their own immune systems, which decreases the chance for infections before or after birth.

HIV is the biggest contributor to maternal deaths in South Africa. Almost a third of pregnant women who visit antenatal clinics in South Africa are HIV-positive.

Second, early attendance allows doctors to treat and manage other treatable health conditions that the mother-to-be may develop. These include high blood pressure and anaemia, which are also major risk factors for maternal deaths.

How Pregnancy Policy Must Change

If late pregnancy recognition is one of the major reasons for late attendance, what does this mean for policy about pregnancy care in South Africa?

There are two policy changes that could rectify this.

First, the National Department of Health needs to make it easier for women to recognise pregnancy. Urine pregnancy tests should be as widely available as condoms.

If women realised that they were pregnant sooner it would improve early antenatal care attendance and enable them to make more informed choices. For example, they would have time to consider an abortion in the case of an unplanned pregnancy.

Second, the way contraception is provided at clinics has to be reconsidered. Four in five women in our study said they had an unplanned pregnancy. The current system, where women can receive contraceptives at clinics, does not have the intended effect of preventing pregnancies. This could be due to the large focus on HIV prevention, which may limit some of the policy attention provided to contraception.

If this system were changed, women would be able to make better choices for themselves and their children.

Implementing these measures could go a long way to improve maternal health and ensure fewer children grow up without their mothers.

In the Dominican Republic High Numbers of Maternal Deaths Plague the Health System

Tarryn Mento

In the following viewpoint, Tarryn Mento details the high rates of maternal mortality in the Dominican Republic, where the lifetime risk of maternal death is one in 320, according to the United Nations Children's Fund (UNICEF). Mento tells the story of a boy named Abraham, who was delivered via Cesarean section at a hospital in the capital of the Dominican Republic. His mother, Nana Charlie, died from maternal hemorrhaging, which is one of the primary reasons for the country's high mortality rate. One of the other reasons why the mortality rate is so high is that hospitals in the Dominican Republic also treat women from Haiti, where the mortality rate is three times higher than it is in the Dominican Republic. Tarryn Mento has a master's degree from the Walter Cronkite School of Journalism and Mass Communication at Arizona State University. She is the Speak City Heights reporter for KPBS in San Diego.

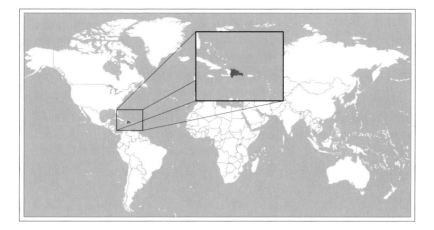

As you read, consider the following questions:

1. Why do hospitals in the Dominican Republic have to handle between 12,000 to 13,000 births annually?

2. How does the Dominican Republic's open-door policy impact how women receive treatment in both the D.R. and Haiti?

3. What impacts does the language barrier have on the ability for doctors to provide treatment to Haitian patients in the Dominican Republic?

A braham's mother was just 17 when she died. The same day that he came into this world was the day she left.

Abraham was delivered by Cesarean section at Hospital Materno-Infantil San Lorenzo de Los Mina, a bustling public hospital in the Dominican capital city. His mother, Nana Charlie, died from excessive bleeding.

Maternal hemorrhaging is one of the main reasons for the Dominican Republic's relatively high maternal mortality rate.

But many come too late. In the Dominican Republic, the lifetime risk of maternal death is one in 320, according to UNICEF. That's almost seven times higher than in the U.S.

Medical experts say a high maternal mortality rate usually correlates to limited medical access. But in the Dominican Republic, skilled medical personnel attend nearly 98 percent of births, only one percentage point less than in this country.

So many women die in childbirth in the Dominican Republic not because they can't get to a doctor, but because they get there so late—and because they come in such great numbers.

"These hospitals are free," said Los Mina Hospital Director Pablo Wagner. "And because they are free, people come from everywhere, from all the surrounding villages."

Wagner said the hospital is equipped to handle 1,500 to 2,000 births a year. Instead, it is handling 12,000 to 13,000 births annually. Many of the mothers are poor, undocumented women who have had little or no prenatal care. Many of these are from Haiti, where the maternal death rate is even worse—three times higher than in the Dominican Republic.

Those are the facts Los Mina deals with every day. So is this one: 24 mothers died in childbirth at the hospital last year. That's about the same number of deaths per 100,000 live births in the U.S.

To medical professionals in the Dominican Republic, health care is a human right. No woman in need of maternal care will be turned away, regardless of her immigration status or ability to pay.

"We have had always an open door policy that we would take anyone who comes," said Leonard Ziur, a Los Mina doctor from Cuba who has also practiced in Miami. "We don't send them back."

Haitians Flood System

Three strangers and their newborns, just hours old, share a bare, dimly lit room at Los Mina. Water leaks onto the tile floor.

Yirandy Contrera sits on a narrow hospital bed, wearing a pink cotton baby doll dress, her inflated belly still visible beneath the thin fabric. Her newborn son, wrapped in white terrycloth embroidered with his name, lies on the mattress next to her.

There is no recognizable chime of a hospital gadget monitoring vitals. No hospital bracelets or visitors' badges. No call button to ensure a nurse is just a ring away. There are just the familiar cries of infants and the comforting coos of their mothers.

The care is mediocre by U.S. standards, but it is far superior to what is available in neighboring Haiti, and, as a result, pregnant Haitian women regularly cross the border illegally into the Dominican Republic to have their babies.

No one knows how many of them come—only that it's many and that the numbers have grown substantially since last year's devastating earthquake in Haiti, which destroyed many hospitals.

"The cost of this hasn't been estimated because there isn't a system that counts the total number of Haitian citizens who live in this country," said Jose Delancer, director of the Department of Women and Children within the Dominican Ministry of Public Health. "How do you count an illegal population, a population that is registered nowhere?"

"The Dominican laws and the Constitution of the Republic guarantee universal access to health care to anyone, no matter their descent, their races, their nationalities, their immigration status," Delancer added. "We as a health care system are not here to question immigration policies. We are here simply to provide quality services to the extent that our capacities allow us to, to anyone who asks for it."

Delancer said the Dominican government has budgeted for public health services for 7 million people in a country with a population of 10 million, although wealthier segments of the population mainly use private health care. The undocumented Haitian population is estimated to represent at least a tenth of the population, some who enter the Dominican solely to deliver their babies.

Many of them have never had a pre-natal check-up, and, as a result, doctors are often unable to anticipate problems and are unprepared for complications that could have been prevented.

Approximately one third of Los Mina patients are Haitian and arrive in poor health, said Wagner, the Los Mina hospital director.

"They don't have a monthly examination, and when they come to the hospital, they come in an awful condition, in a bad situation," he said. "They are mothers that don't have the proper conditions to support nine months of pregnancy. They are without nutrition, without education."

Abraham's mother was one such patient, according to local religious leader Malia Duval and other members of the community who are familiar with the case. When she arrived at the hospital to give birth, she was in poor condition. She was undernourished and battling sickle-cell anemia and wasn't strong enough to survive surgery. She bled to death after undergoing a Cesarean section.

Language Barriers

More than five months after the death of his mother, Abraham sleeps on a bed in a home in Batey San Isidro, an impoverished community made up mostly of Haitian immigrants on the outskirts of Santo Domingo. Flies drift freely around his head.

With the whereabouts of their father unknown, Abraham and his 2-year-old sister, Annabelle, live in the care of Eriana Alce, a neighbor of their deceased mother. At 23, Eriana is four months pregnant and already has two children of her own. One of them, a toddler, sits on the dirty cement floor, biting and occasionally swallowing pieces of a torn plastic bag.

An immigrant from Haiti, Eriana does not have Dominican citizenship and can't legally work. Her husband works at a nightclub, but the couple struggle to feed the children they have.

Asked what she is going to do with another baby coming, Eriana replies, "Nada."

There is nothing she can do.

Like many immigrants from Haiti, Eriana speaks only a little Spanish. Her native language is a dialect of French-Creole, and that presents yet another challenge to health care professionals.

"Usually they come when they are almost at time of delivery," said Ziur, the Cuban doctor at Los Mina. "They live in Haiti. They get here and they tell you, 'No, I don't speak Spanish. I don't speak English. I don't speak anything, only Creole.'"

Translators are sometimes available at the hospital, but not always. Ziur said he handles an average of 40 patients a day. In a typical eight-hour day, that's five patients per hour, and nearly one third do not speak Spanish.

The Dominican Ministry of Public Health is trying to overcome the language problems by adopting a common form for perinatal histories and translating it into Creole. The ministry has disseminated the translated document throughout Dominican hospitals and also has sent the form to Haiti.

Common Problems

The maternal health problems in the Dominican Republic are not unique, and, in fact, many are the same as those facing immigrant populations in the U.S.

Many undocumented women in the U.S. have little or no access to pre-natal care during pregnancy, according to a 2010 Amnesty International report. Private insurance is too expensive, and they don't qualify for Medicaid because they are in the country unlawfully.

Although U.S. law requires that all women in active labor have access to medical care regardless of immigration status, many arrive at hospitals in poor condition, according to the report. They frequently lack pre-natal care and don't speak the language.

Medical care for undocumented immigrants is being increasingly debated in the U.S. In Arizona, for example, a bill introduced in the state Legislature last year would have required hospitals to identify suspected illegal immigrants. While those in need of emergency services would get them, the bill would have denied services to others.

The bill failed to pass after hospital and medical associations voiced strong opposition to checking patients' immigration status. However, state Sen. Steve Smith, a Republican who represents a large district south and east of Phoenix, has said he intends to reintroduce the bill next session.

Such a debate has not yet surfaced in the Dominican Republic, despite evidence that treating illegal immigrants has stretched the health care system beyond its capabilities and even though the two countries—the Dominican and Haiti—have a long history of antagonistic relations.

Ziur is typical of doctors who say that if the Dominican Republic adopted a law requiring hospitals to notify authorities of a patient's immigration status, he would refuse.

Treating undocumented population may be hurting the Dominican health care system, but not treating people in need would be more painful.

"I will not do it. I will just resist," he said.

Medical care, he said, is not about policy or politics.

"Your duty's not that. I'm here to save lives."

Periodical and Internet Sources Bibliography

The following articles have been selected to supplement the diverse views presented in this chapter.

EAEF, "Young Women Are Now a 'High-Risk Group' for Mental Illness," Egyptian American Enterprise Fund. https://eaef.org/young-women-are-now-a-high-risk-group-for-mental-illness/.

Editorial, "Are Young Women More Prone to Mental Health Issues?" Laguna Treatment Hospital, January 31, 2019. https://lagunatreatment.com/support-for-women/mental-health-issues/.

Genomind, "The 8 Most Common Mental Health Issues Affecting Young Women," Genomind, March 2, 2018. https://genomind.com/8-common-mental-health-issues-affecting-young-women/.

Laura Greenstein, "What To Do If Your Workplace Is Anxiety-Inducing," National Alliance on Mental Illness, February 22, 2018. https://www.nami.org/Blogs/NAMI-Blog/February-2018/What-To-Do-if-Your-Workplace-is-Anxiety-Inducing.

Nicole Karlis, "New research reveals how sexism in healthcare can literally kill women," Salon, December 14, 2018. https://www.salon.com/2018/12/14/new-research-reveals-how-sexism-in-healthcare-can-literally-kill-women/.

Nicole Lyn Pesce, "These are the signs that your job is making you seriously depressed," MarketWatch, August 15, 2017. https://www.marketwatch.com/story/these-are-the-signs-that-your-job-is-making-you-seriously-depressed-2017-08-15.

Kayla Platoff, "First, Do No Harm (To Men)," StudyBreaks, May 22, 2018. https://studybreaks.com/news-politics/sexism-health-care-women/.

Robert Powell 7 A. Pawlowski, "Gender bias in health care may be harming women's health: What you need to know," Today, July 18, 2018. https://www.today.com/health/gender-bias-health-care-may-be-harming-women-s-health-t133583.

Charming Peries, "U.S. Gag Rule Expansion Will Constrain Women's Rights Worldwide," Real News Network, April 26, 2019. https://

therealnews.com/stories/u-s-gag-rule-expansion-will-constrain-womens-rights-worldwide.

Christine Ro, "The Global Gag Rule On Abortion Is Counterproductive," *Forbes*, May 1, 2019. https://www.forbes.com/sites/christinero/2019/05/01/the-global-gag-rule-on-abortion-is-counterproductive/#4901cb901815.

Lauren Sega, "Ohioans Fight Back Against Global Gag Rule," Columbus Underground, May 8, 2019. https://www.columbusunderground.com/ohioans-fight-back-against-global-gag-rule.

Pooja Shah, "Haiti's Maternal Health Crisis," International Policy Digest, March 3, 2018. https://intpolicydigest.org/2018/03/03/haiti-s-maternal-health-crisis/.

Nick Triggle, "Mental health: One in four young women struggling," BBC News, November 22, 2018. https://www.bbc.com/news/health-46295719.

UNFPA, "Slashing Haiti's maternal and infant death rates, one delivery at a time," United Nations Population Fund, February 26, 2015. https://www.unfpa.org/news/slashing-haiti%E2%80%99s-maternal-and-infant-death-rates-one-delivery-time.

For Further Discussion

Chapter 1

1. How has the handling of the spread of HIV/AIDS in the United States informed how treatment is conducted around the world?
2. Was the Zika Virus epidemic blown out of proportion leading up to the 2016 Olympics? Why or why not?

Chapter 2

1. Why do people often follow the uninformed medical advice from celebrities instead of their own doctors?
2. How can medical professionals counter misinformation?

Chapter 3

1. How can mental health be better factored into disaster response?
2. What are ways to lessen the stigma around mental illness around the world?

Chapter 4

1. What are ways to lessen the sexism that is rampant in the healthcare industry?
2. Why are maternal mortality rates high around the world, even in a rich country like the United States?

Organizations to Contact

The editors have compiled the following list of organizations concerned with the issues debated in this book. The descriptions are derived from materials provided by the organizations. All have publications or information available for interested readers. The list was compiled on the date of publication of the present volume; the information provided here may change. Be aware that many organizations take several weeks or longer to respond to inquiries, so allow as much time as possible.

American Psychological Association
750 First St. NE, Washington, DC 20002-4242
(800) 374-2721
email: jboston@apa.org
website: www.apa.org/

APA is the leading scientific and professional organization representing psychology in the United States, with more than 118,000 researchers, educators, clinicians, consultants and students as its members. Our mission is to promote the advancement, communication, and application of psychological science and knowledge to benefit society and improve lives.

Amnesty International
1 Easton St, London WC1X 0DW, UK
+44 20 7413 5500
email: careers@amnesty.org
website: www.amnesty.org

Amnesty International is a global movement of more than 7 million people who take injustice personally. We are campaigning for a world where human rights are enjoyed by all. We are funded by members and people like you. We are independent of any political ideology, economic interest or religion. No government is beyond scrutiny. No situation is beyond hope. Few would have predicted when we started that torturers would become international outlaws. That most countries would abolish the death penalty. And seemingly untouchable dictators would be made to answer for their crimes.

Anxiety and Depression Association of America
8701 Georgia Ave Suite 412, Silver Spring, MD 20910
(240) 485-1001
email: information@adaa.org
website: https://adaa.org/

ADAA focuses on improving quality of life for those with these disorders. ADAA provides education about the disorders and helps people find treatment, resources, and support. More than 38 million people visit ADAA's website each year - from all across the globe. ADAA strives to improve patient care by promoting implementation of evidence-based treatments and best practices across disciplines through continuing education and trainings and accelerating dissemination of research into practice. ADAA promotes scientific innovation and engages a diverse network of basic and clinical anxiety and depression researchers and providers encouraging the implementation of new treatments to clinicians. These commitments drive ADAA's promise to find new treatments and one day prevent and cure these disorders.

Doctors Without Borders (USA)
40 Rector St, 16th Floor, New York, NY 10006
(212) 679-6800
email: jessica.brown@newyork.msf.org
website: www.doctorswithoutborders.org

Every day, our teams deliver emergency medical aid to those who need it most. As we carry out this work, we are guided by the rules of medical ethics—particularly the duty to provide care without causing harm to individuals or groups. We're also committed to safeguarding our patients' rights to autonomy, confidentiality, and informed consent. We respect the dignity of our patients, which includes respect for their cultural and religious beliefs. In accordance with these principles, we endeavor to provide the best medical care possible to all patients.

International AIDS Society
Avenue de France 23, CH-1202, Geneva, Switzerland
+41 22 710 0800
email: info@iasociety.org
website: www.iasociety.org/

The mission of the International AIDS Society (IAS) is to lead collective action on every front of the global HIV response through its membership base, scientific authority, and convening power. Founded in 1988, the IAS is the world's largest association of HIV professionals, with members from more than 180 countries working on all fronts of the global AIDS response. Together, we advocate and drive urgent action to reduce the global impact of HIV.

International Women's Health Coalition
333 Seventh Ave, New York City, NY 10001
(212) 979-8500
email: info@iwhc.org
website: www.iwhc.org

IWHC advances the sexual and reproductive health and rights of women and young people, particularly adolescent girls, in Africa, Asia, Eastern Europe, Latin America, and the Middle East. IWHC furthers this agenda by supporting and strengthening leaders and organizations working at the community, national, regional, and global levels, and by advocating for international and U.S. policies, programs, and funding. IWHC builds bridges between local realities and international policy by connecting women and young people in the Global South to key decision-makers. In doing so, IWHC brings local voices to global debates and in turn, makes global processes and policies more understandable and actionable at the local level.

Joint United Nations Programme on HIV/AIDS

20 Avenue Appia, CH-1211 Geneva 27, Switzerland
+41 22 791 36 66
email: aidsinfo@unaids.org
website: www.unaids.org

Since the first cases of HIV were reported more than 35 years ago, 78 million people have become infected with HIV and 35 million have died from AIDS-related illnesses. Since it started operations in 1996, UNAIDS has led and inspired global, regional, national and local leadership, innovation and partnership to ultimately consign HIV to history. UNAIDS is a problem-solver. It places people living with HIV and people affected by the virus at the decision-making table and at the centre of designing, delivering and monitoring the AIDS response. It charts paths for countries and communities to get on the Fast-Track to ending AIDS and is a bold advocate for addressing the legal and policy barriers to the AIDS response.

Mental Health Foundation

Colechurch House, 1 London Bridge Walk, London SE1 2SX
+44 (0) 20 7803 1100
email: press@mentalhealth.org.uk
website: www.mentalhealth.org.uk

The Mental Health Foundation is the UK's charity for everyone's mental health. With prevention at the heart of what we do, we aim to find and address the sources of mental health problems. We must make the same progress for the health of our minds that we have achieved for the health of our bodies. And when we do, we will look back and think that this was our time's greatest contribution to human flourishing. The Mental Health Foundation is a UK charity that relies on public donations and grant funding to deliver and campaign for good mental health for all.

National Alliance on Mental Illness

3803 N Fairfax Dr, Suite 100, Arlington, VA 22203
(703) 524-7600
email: info@nami.org
website: www.nami.org

We educate. Offered in thousands of communities across the United States through NAMI State Organizations and NAMI Affiliates, our education programs ensure hundreds of thousands of families, individuals and educators get the support and information they need. We advocate. NAMI shapes national public policy for people with mental illness and their families and provides volunteer leaders with the tools, resources and skills necessary to save mental health in all states. We listen. Our toll-free NAMI HelpLine allows us to respond personally to hundreds of thousands of requests each year, providing free information and support—a much-needed lifeline for many.

National Institute of Mental Health and Neuro-Sciences

Hosur Road, Bangalore - 560029, India
+91 80 2699 5530
email: info@nimhans.ac.in
website: www.nimhans.ac.in

To be a world leader in the area of Mental Health and Neurosciences and evolve state-of-the-art approaches to patient care through translational research. Establish the highest standards of evidence-based care for psychiatric and neurological disorders and rehabilitation. Develop expertise and set standards of care for diseases of public health relevance in the developing world. Work with the government and provide consultancy services for policy planning and monitoring strategies in the field of Mental Health and Neurosciences and facilitate execution of national health programme. Human resource capacity building by training in diverse fields related to Mental Health and Neurosciences. Develop and strengthen inter-disciplinary, inter-institutional and international collaboration with universities and research institutes across the globe to foster scientific research, training in advanced technology and exchange of ideas in the areas of Mental Health and Neurosciences.

The United Nations
760 United Nations Plaza, New York City, NY 10017
(212) 963-8687
email: info@un.org
website: www.un.org

Due to the powers vested in its Charter and its unique international character, the United Nations can take action on the issues confronting humanity in the 21st century, such as peace and security, climate change, sustainable development, human rights, disarmament, terrorism, humanitarian and health emergencies, gender equality, governance, food production, and more.

United Nations Children's Fund (UNICEF)
125 Maiden Lane, 11th Floor, New York, NY 10038
(212) 686-5522
email: info@unicefusa.org
website: www.unicef.org

UNICEF promotes the rights and wellbeing of every child, in everything we do. Together with our partners, we work in 190 countries and territories to translate that commitment into practical action, focusing special effort on reaching the most vulnerable and excluded children, to the benefit of all children, everywhere. In all of its work, UNICEF takes a life-cycle based approach, recognizing the particular importance of early childhood development and adolescence. UNICEF programmes focus on the most disadvantaged children, including those living in fragile contexts, those with disabilities, those who are affected by rapid urbanization and those affected by environmental degradation.

United Nations High Commissioner for Refugees

Case Postale 2500 CH-1211 Geneve 2 Depot, Suisse
+41 22 739 8111
email: info@unhcr.org
website: www.unhcr.org

During times of displacement, we provide critical emergency assistance in the form of clean water, sanitation and healthcare, as well as shelter, blankets, household goods and sometimes food. We also arrange transport and assistance packages for people who return home, and income-generating projects for those who resettle.

World Health Organization (WHO)

Avenue Appia 20, 1202 Geneva, Switzerland
+41 22 791 2111
email: mediainquiries@who.int
website: www.who.int

WHO works worldwide to promote health, keep the world safe, and serve the vulnerable. Our goal is to ensure that a billion more people have universal health coverage, to protect a billion more people from health emergencies, and provide a further billion people with better health and well-being.

Bibliography of Books

Vincanne Adams. *Metrics: What Counts in Global Health (Critical Global Health: Evidence, Efficacy, Ethnography).* Durham, NC: Duke University Press, 2016.

Joseph Alton, MD. *The Zika Virus Handbook: A Doctor Explains All You Need To Know About The Pandemic.* Weston, Fl: Doom 7 Bloom LLC, 2016.

Diana Lynn Barnes. *Women's Reproductive Mental Health Across the Lifespan.* New York, NY: Springer Publishing, 2015.

Stephan Bauman, Matthew Soerens, Dr. Issam Smeir. *Seeking Refuge: On the Shores of the Global Refugee Crisis.* Chicago, IL: Moody Pubishers, 2016.

R. E. Black, R. Laxminarayan, M. Temmerman, et al., editors. *Reproductive, Maternal, Newborn, and Child Health: Disease Control Priorities, Third Edition (Volume 2).* Washington, DC: National Institute of Health, 2016.

Chelsea Clinton, Devi Sridhar. *Governing Global Health: Who Runs the World and Why?* Oxford, United Kingdom: Oxford University Press, 2017.

Svea Closser. *Chasing Polio in Pakistan: Why the World's Largest Public Health Initiative May Fail.* Nashville, TN: Vanderbilt University Press, 2010.

Donald G. McNeil Jr. *Zika: The Emerging Epidemic.* New York, NY: W.W. Norton & Company, 2016.

Michael H. Merson, Robert E Black, Anne J Mills. *Global Health: Diseases, Programs, Systems, and Policies.* Burlington, MA: Jones & Bartlett Learning: 2018.

Paul Offit, MD. *Bad Advice: Or Why Celebrities, Politicians, and Activists Aren't Your Best Source of Health Information.* New York, NY: Columbia University Press, 2018.

Randall M Packard. *A History of Global Health: Interventions into the Lives of Other Peoples*. Baltimore, MD: Johns Hopkins University Press, 2016.

Kiran Pienaar. *Politics in the Making of HIV/AIDS in South Africa*. London, United Kingdom: Plagrave Macmillan, 2016.

Yana van der Meulen Rodgers. *The Global Gag Rule and Women's Reproductive Health: Rhetoric Versus Reality*. Oxford, UK: Oxford University Press, 2018.

Nina Shapiro, MD, and Kristin Loberg. *Hype: A Doctor's Guide to Medical Myths, Exaggerated Claims, and Bad Advice - How to Tell What's Real and What's Not*. New York, NY: St. Martin's Press, 2018.

Dr. Suzanne Steinbaum. *Dr. Suzanne Steinbaum's Heart Book: Every Woman's Guide to a Heart-Healthy Life*. New York, NY: Avery Publishing, 2014.

Carolyn Thomas. *A Woman's Guide to Living with Heart Disease*. Baltimore, MD: Johns Hopkins University Press, 2017.

Index

K

Kassam, Ashifa, 30–34
Komproe, Ivan H., 102–113
Kovind, Ram Nath, 127

L

Lewis, Taylor, 147–156
Lluveras, Lauren, 35–40
Luitel, Nagendra P., 102–113
Lyme disease, 22

M

malaria, 22, 23
Marcovitch, Harvey, 58–65
Mawarpury, Marty, 133
measles, mumps, and rubella
   (MMR) vaccine, 15, 58–65
measles outbreaks, 60–61, 70
Medicaid, 38
medical innovation, 15–16,
   41–48
medical supply distribution,
   and use of drones, 41,
   43–44
Menne, Bettina, 19–23
mental health, social
   stigmatization of, 93–101,
   102–113
Mental Health Care Act
   (India), 131
Mento, Tarryn, 178–184
Mexico City Policy, 147–156

mosquito-borne diseases, 22,
   30–34
Murch, Simon, 63

N

National Immunization Days
   (NIDs), 74
Nepal, mental health
   treatment in, 102–113
Nigeria, 14, 28, 32, 72–80, 104

O

Office of Research Integrity,
   58, 60
Olympic Games, 14, 30–34
Omaar, Abbas, 27
O'Sullivan, Chris, 135–143

P

Pai, Mallesh, 93–101
Pakistan, polio outbreaks, in,
   72–80
Patel, Vikram, 131
Peru, reproductive rights in,
   147–156
Physicians for Human Rights
   (PHR), 49, 50, 53
polio, 72–80
post-surgical care, 44–45
post-traumatic stress disorder,
   15
pre-exposure prophylaxis, 26